Scratch & Play

⇾ TEST YOUR ⇽
BLACK
JACK
IQ

ANDREW BRISMAN

PUZZLE
WRIGHT
PRESS

New York

PUZZLE WRIGHT PRESS

New York

An Imprint of Sterling Publishing
387 Park Avenue South
New York, NY 10016

ISBN 978-1-4027-8156-8

Distributed in Canada by Sterling Publishing
ᶜ/o Canadian Manda Group, 165 Dufferin Street
Toronto, Ontario, Canada M6K 3H6
Distributed in the United Kingdom by GMC Distribution Services
Castle Place, 166 High Street, Lewes, East Sussex, England BN7 1XU
Distributed in Australia by Capricorn Link (Australia) Pty. Ltd.
P.O. Box 704, Windsor, NSW 2756, Australia

For information about custom editions, special sales, and premium and
corporate purchases, please contact Sterling Special Sales at 800-805-5489
or specialsales@sterlingpublishing.com.

Printed in China

2 4 6 8 10 9 7 5 3 1

CONTENTS

INTRODUCTION

Blackjack is a game of skill. Unlike most other casino games, blackjack allows the player to make meaningful decisions. The correct rules for decision-making are collectively known as basic strategy.

If you want to play smart blackjack, you need to know basic strategy. Intelligent players use it to shave the house's advantage to a fraction of a percent. So what's your basic strategy IQ? That's what you're here to find out.

In all likelihood, you're already familiar with basic strategy. You bought this book to sharpen and test your skills. Good. Jump into the hands right after you read the instructions on how to play. Of course, I recommend reading the rest of the book as well. It will help deepen your understanding and appreciation of basic strategy.

Or perhaps you're a novice blackjack player—even a regular player—and you're only vaguely familiar with basic strategy. You know it's supposed to improve your results and help you win, but you haven't yet absorbed it. This book is also for you. Read the first sections that ground you in basic strategy, learn the chart found on the inside covers and page 88 (it's not nearly as daunting as you may think), and then give the IQ test a go. You'll soon discover which decisions you know down cold and which ones trip you up.

This book will not teach you the basic rules of blackjack—it assumes you know the mechanics of the game. If you need to learn how to play, you can find the rules online. (Or might I humbly suggest you pick up my own *Mensa Guide to Casino Gambling*?) Nor does this book teach you how to "beat" blackjack. You can't do that unless you count cards and that's a much more demanding and complex skill set than basic strategy alone. But don't lose heart: basic strategy can have you playing almost even with the house.

Most people who play blackjack regularly claim they know basic strategy. Yet many of these players are sorely mistaken. Yes, they may know *how* to stand, hit, split, surrender, and double down. But that doesn't mean they know *when* to stand, hit, split, surrender, and double down. Think you know better? If you're itching to find out, start scratching.

—Andrew Brisman

HOW TO TAKE
THE BLACKJACK IQ TEST

The basic strategy IQ test consists of 406 hands. For each hand, you are shown the dealer's upcard and your first two or three cards. (Three cards mean, of course, that the hand has already received a hit.) You must then scratch off your decision: hit, stand, double, surrender, or split. Double and surrender are available for two-card hands only, with split replacing surrender as an option when the first two cards are a pair. (In case you're wondering, you would never surrender a pair under the test's playing conditions.)

A correct decision is indicated by a +. An incorrect decision is indicated by an ×. Hands are not played until resolution; they are played only until you make the correct basic strategy decision.

For these hands, you are playing under the following conditions:

- Multiple decks (i.e., four to eight decks)
- Dealer stands on soft 17*
- Double down on any two cards
- Double after splitting allowed
- Surrender allowed

You'll find the basic strategy chart for these conditions on page 88 and on the inside covers. Don't use the chart while taking the test—that would defeat the purpose of measuring your basic strategy know-how.

When you are finished with the IQ test, total all the hands you got wrong—meaning the ones where you didn't reveal the + on your first attempt. Of course, you're aiming for a perfect score, but if you missed five or fewer, consider yourself a basic strategy whiz. If you did play perfectly, congratulations—the house has only a tiny 0.4% edge against you. It doesn't get much better than that.

You don't need to keep buying the book until you get a perfect score (although you're welcome to!). You may want to create flash-cards of the hands that led to errors or where you felt you were

---

*Although games in which the dealer hits soft 17 are becoming commonplace, I opted for the more player-favorable rule of standing on soft 17. (Note: It's a more favorable rule only when all else is equal. See the discussion of rule variations on page 34.)

guessing. Drill yourself on these hands again and again until you're confident you know the correct play.

Unlike a typical computer blackjack game, the IQ test is designed to present every nontrivial hand—including those that occur less frequently but present some of the most difficult decisions (i.e., soft hands and splits). No significant decision is left out; if you have a weakness in your basic strategy, it will come to light.

You may notice that there are no three-card low hands. With three cards, the choices are just hit and stand, and if you have 11 or less, a hit can't hurt you. In fact, many dealers will automatically keep hitting until you get at least 12.

Similarly, you won't see every three-card soft hand of 16 or below (though you'll see many of them). You're always going to hit with these hands; there's a good chance the card will be coming out of the dealer's hand before you even make the official signal. (You also always hit a three-card soft 17, but you'll be tested here against every dealer's upcard to make sure you don't forget!)

You'll see only a sample of other no-brainers: two-card hard 18–20 and three-card 18–20. And, sorry to say, you won't be dealt any blackjack hands, the best no-brainers of them all. I hope you receive tons of them at the casino, but since they require no basic strategy decisions, they don't appear in the test.

Good luck on the test—and best of luck at the tables.

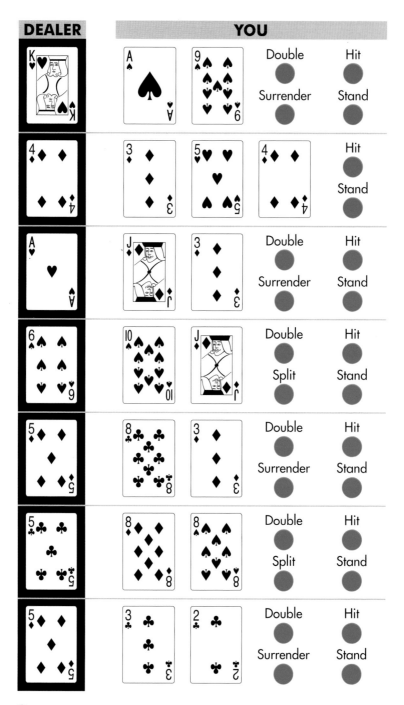

DEALER	YOU			
K♥	A♠	9♥	Double / Surrender	Hit / Stand
4♦	3♦	5♥	4♦	Hit / Stand
A♥	J♦	3♦	Double / Surrender	Hit / Stand
6♠	10♠	J♦	Double / Split	Hit / Stand
5♦	8♣	3♦	Double / Surrender	Hit / Stand
5♣	8♦	8♠	Double / Split	Hit / Stand
5♦	3♣	2♣	Double / Surrender	Hit / Stand

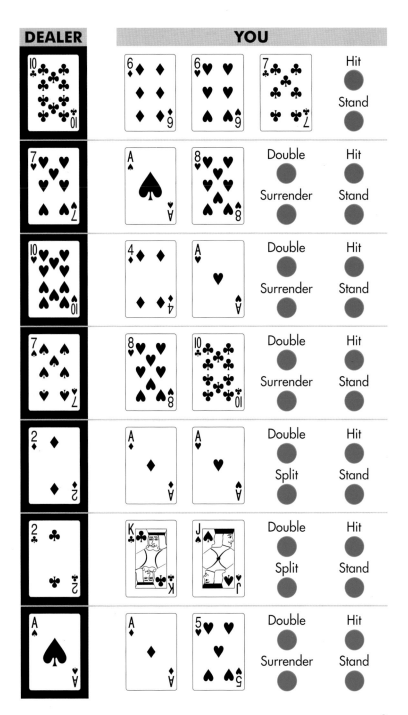

DEALER	YOU			
10♣	6♦ 9	6♥ 9	7♣ 7	Hit / Stand
7♥	A♠	8♥	Double / Surrender	Hit / Stand
10♥	4♦	A♥	Double / Surrender	Hit / Stand
7♠	8♥	10♣	Double / Surrender	Hit / Stand
2♦	A♦	A♥	Double / Split	Hit / Stand
2♣	K♣	J♠	Double / Split	Hit / Stand
A♠	A♦	5♥	Double / Surrender	Hit / Stand

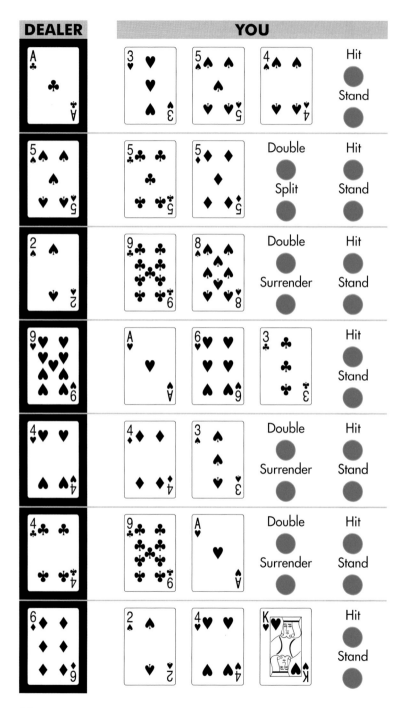

DEALER	YOU			
5♦	3♦	5♠	A♣	Hit / Stand
8♦	Q♠	3♠	5♦	Hit / Stand
5♥	A♥	A♠		Double / Hit / Split / Stand
3♠	5♠	2♥	K♠	Hit / Stand
2♦	K♦	8♥		Double / Hit / Surrender / Stand
9♣	J♥	4♥		Double / Hit / Surrender / Stand
5♠	10♦	9♠		Double / Hit / Surrender / Stand

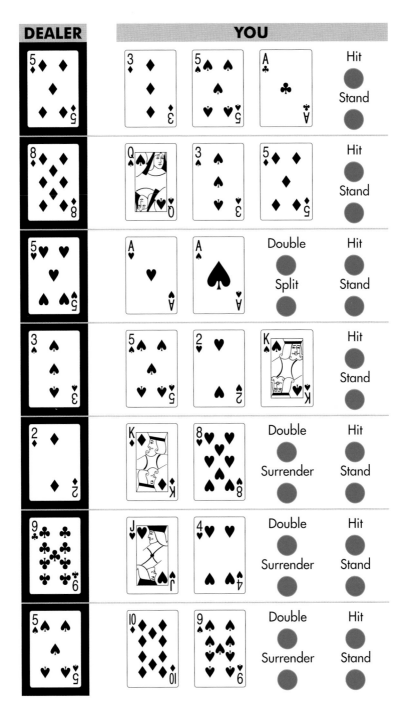

11

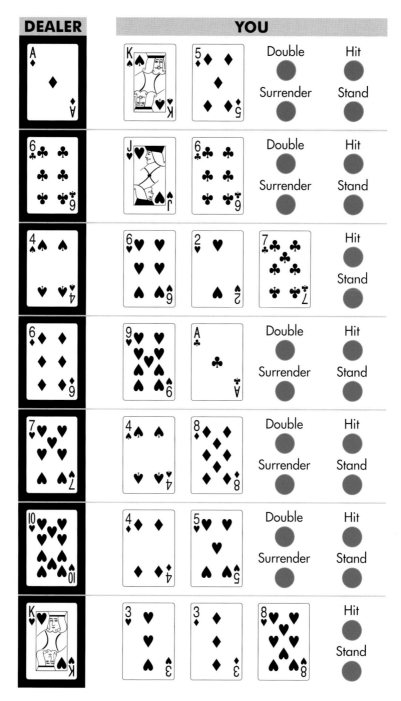

DEALER	YOU			
A♦	K♠	5♦	Double Surrender	Hit Stand
6♣	J♥	6♣	Double Surrender	Hit Stand
4♠	6♥	2♥	7♣	Hit Stand
6♦	9♥	A♣	Double Surrender	Hit Stand
7♥	4♠	8♦	Double Surrender	Hit Stand
10♥	4♦	5♥	Double Surrender	Hit Stand
K♥	3♥	3♦	8♥	Hit Stand

12

DEALER	YOU			

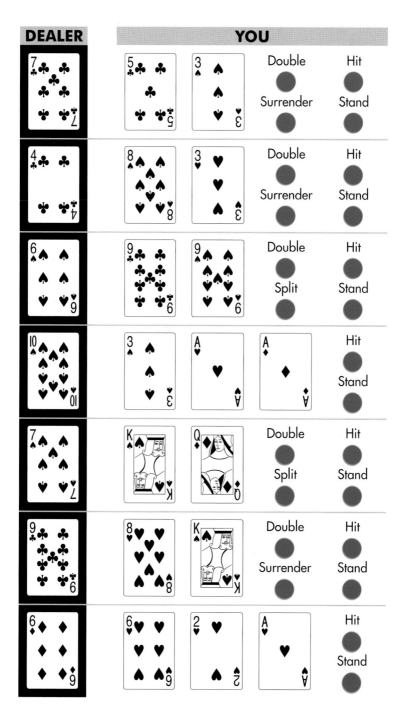

13

DEALER	YOU			

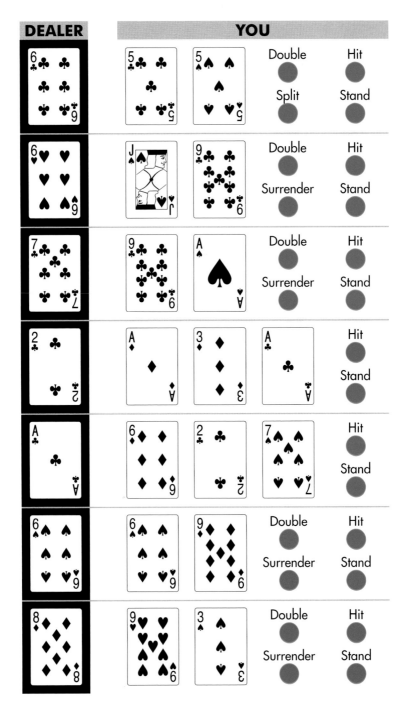

6♣ / **5♣ 5♠** — Double · Hit · Split · Stand

6♥ / **J♠ 9♣** — Double · Hit · Surrender · Stand

7♣ / **9♣ A♠** — Double · Hit · Surrender · Stand

2♣ / **A♦ 3♦ A♣** — Hit · Stand

A♣ / **6♦ 2♣ 7♠** — Hit · Stand

6♠ / **6♠ 9♦** — Double · Hit · Surrender · Stand

8♦ / **9♥ 3♠** — Double · Hit · Surrender · Stand

14

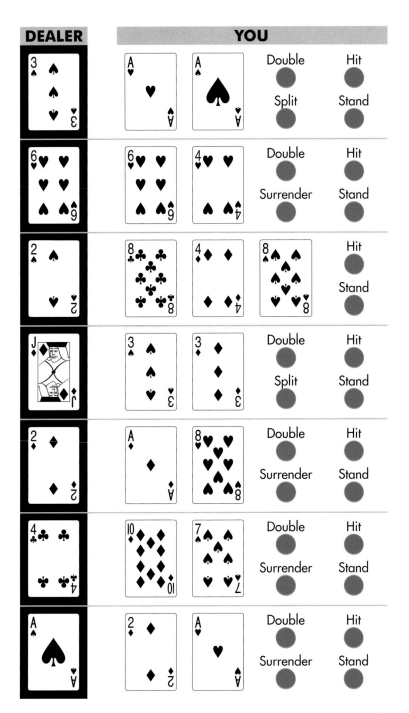

BASIC TRAINING

If you're not already comfortable with basic strategy, how do you learn it so it becomes second nature? You need to get very cozy with the strategy chart appropriate to the game you're playing. For the IQ test in this book, the chart is on page 88 and on both inside covers.

To read the chart, you find the dealer's upcard at the top of each section, and your hand along the left side. At the intersection is the action you should take. Treat two-card and three-card totals the same. (But remember that double, split, and surrender only apply to two-card hands.)

You can master the chart in stages. First learn strategy for the hard hands (hands that do not contain an ace valued as 11), then the split hands (hands that start with a pair), and finally the soft hands (hands where an ace can be valued as 1 or 11). Memorize the decisions. Drill yourself with a deck of cards, or, better yet, flashcards. When you feel fluent in the strategy, use this book as your final exam.

It's very satisfying to know basic strategy cold and play without wavering or hesitation. However, if there are still decisions that stymie you (like when to double those pesky soft totals), there's no shame in tearing off the cover of this book and bringing the strategy chart to the blackjack table. You'll see other players with cards, copies, or printouts. No casino should have a problem with this. Just make sure you don't slow up play by having to refer to the chart all the time. Also, feel free to show your fellow players the cover of the book and recommend it to everyone.

Different Games, Different Strategies
If you ace this book's IQ test, does that mean you've mastered basic strategy for every blackjack game the casino can throw at you? Not quite. Unfortunately, there is no "standard" blackjack game—that is, the rules and conditions can vary. (Read more about the effects of these changes on page 34.) In fact, you can often find several different flavors of blackjack within the same casino, even though they're all simply labeled "blackjack." (I'm not referring to

exotic variations such as Spanish 21 and double exposure black-jack, which feature myriad changes to the game.)

When the blackjack rules change, the basic strategy usually changes as well. Some of the answers on the IQ test would be different if the conditions were changed from multiple decks, dealer stands on soft 17, and double after split allowed to, say, single deck, dealer hits soft 17, and no double after split. Ideally, you should familiarize yourself with the chart particular to the game you play. However, you won't lose much in expectation if you use the multiple-deck strategy as your foundation—probably no more than 0.5 percent. But if you're playing to win and you're a basic strategy buff (which clearly you are!), why sacrifice anything?

Starting on page 88, you can find basic strategy charts for single-deck and multiple-deck games. Double-deck strategy is unique from single- and multiple-deck strategy, but was not included because of space limitations. You can also head online to find charts specific to the blackjack conditions you play. An excellent resource is the Wizard of Odds (wizardofodds.com). The Wizard (a.k.a. actuary and gambling guru Michael Shackleford) offers a basic strategy calculator for a variety of playing conditions; he also supplies plenty of insight into the nuts and bolts of basic strategy.

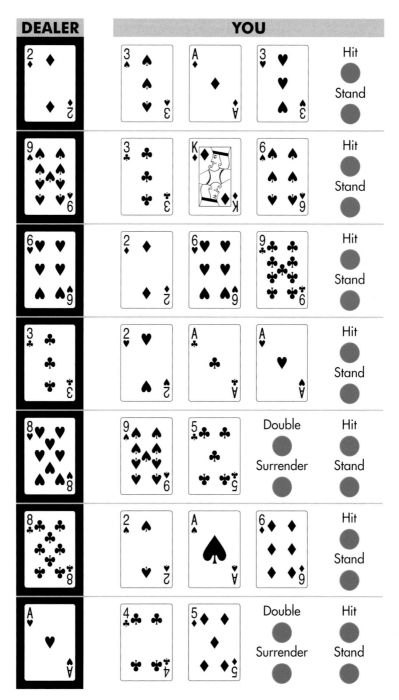

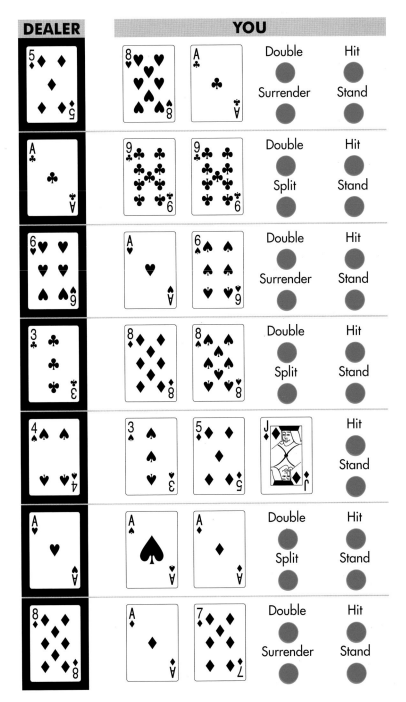

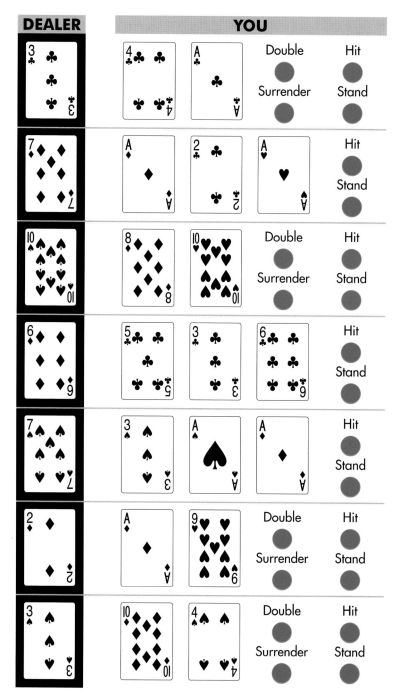

DEALER	YOU			
4♥	A♣	2♠	7♠	**Hit** ● **Stand** ●
J♥	Q♠	7♣	**Double** ● **Surrender** ●	**Hit** ● **Stand** ●
4♥	A♠	2♥	A♦	**Hit** ● **Stand** ●
8♦	3♦	4♣	6♠	**Hit** ● **Stand** ●
6♦	A♠	A♣	**Double** ● **Split** ●	**Hit** ● **Stand** ●
8♠	9♠	A♦	**Double** ● **Surrender** ●	**Hit** ● **Stand** ●
4♦	10♣	K♦	**Double** ● **Split** ●	**Hit** ● **Stand** ●

THE BASIS FOR BASIC STRATEGY

Where does basic strategy come from? It's a reflection of statistical truths. For each hand you hold versus each possible dealer upcard, there exists only one correct action with the highest mathematical expectation. The expectation is calculated inside a vacuum: the only considerations are your cards, the dealer's upcard, and the rules of the game. The other cards in play and the other players are of no account; it's as if you always have a freshly shuffled deck of cards and it's just you and the dealer at the table.

How does one calculate the highest average expected return for each basic strategy decision? Not easily. Each playing decision has been derived and confirmed through calculations using combinatorial analysis and through computer simulations involving the play of millions and millions of hands. For example, if you want to give general advice on what to do with a 13 vs. 7, you have to consider hands of 7–6, 8–5, 9–4, 10–3, 2–3–3–5, etc. Oh yes, and then the results of every possible combination of hits to your cards and to the dealer's cards must be taken into account. Only then can you declare with certainty that you always hit 13 versus a dealer's 7. You do it because it will return more money to you in the long run when compared to standing.

The right decisions will help you make (or save) money while the wrong decisions will cost money. What does this mean in terms of dollars and cents? Let's assume that you play $10 a hand and 100 hands per hour. If you're an average player, you're expected to lose about 2% of what you wager in the long run. If you're a basic strategy player, you can probably knock that down to 0.5%. Those percentages translate to dollars. The average hourly loss for the average player is $20 (100 hands × $10 × 2%). The average hourly loss for the basic strategy player is $5 (100 hands × $10 × 0.5%). That's a $15 difference. In other words, the average player loses four times as much money as the basic strategy buff. (Remember: these are long-term averages, not session-to-session guarantees.)

You'll note that basic strategy works its magic only to a certain degree: you're still playing at a disadvantage. To gain an advantage against the house you would have to count cards, which requires hard work, a thick skin, and a strong bankroll.

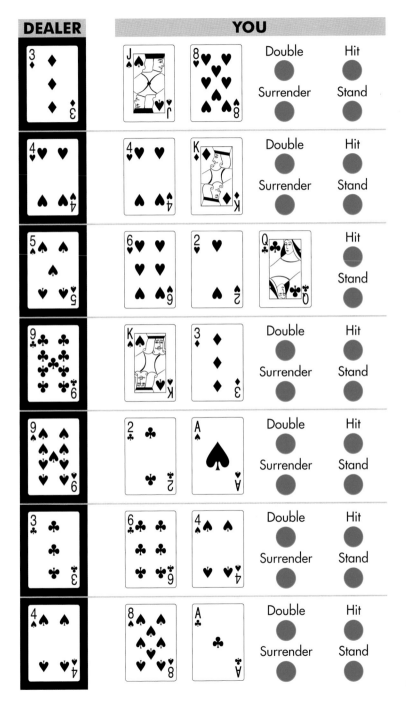

DEALER	YOU			
3♦	J♠	8♥	Double · Surrender	Hit · Stand
4♥	4♥	K♦	Double · Surrender	Hit · Stand
5♠	6♥	2♥	Q♣	Hit · Stand
9♣	K♠	3♦	Double · Surrender	Hit · Stand
9♠	2♣	A♠	Double · Surrender	Hit · Stand
3♣	6♣	4♠	Double · Surrender	Hit · Stand
4♠	8♠	A♣	Double · Surrender	Hit · Stand

23

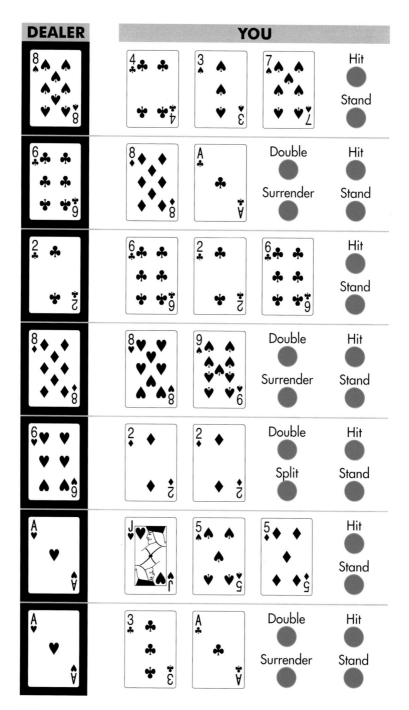

DEALER	YOU			
8♠	4♣	3♠	7♠	Hit / Stand
6♣	8♦	A♣		Double / Hit / Surrender / Stand
2♣	6♣	2♣	6♣	Hit / Stand
8♦	8♥	9♠		Double / Hit / Surrender / Stand
6♥	2♦	2♦		Double / Hit / Split / Stand
A♥	J♥	5♠	5♦	Hit / Stand
A♥	3♣	A♣		Double / Hit / Surrender / Stand

24

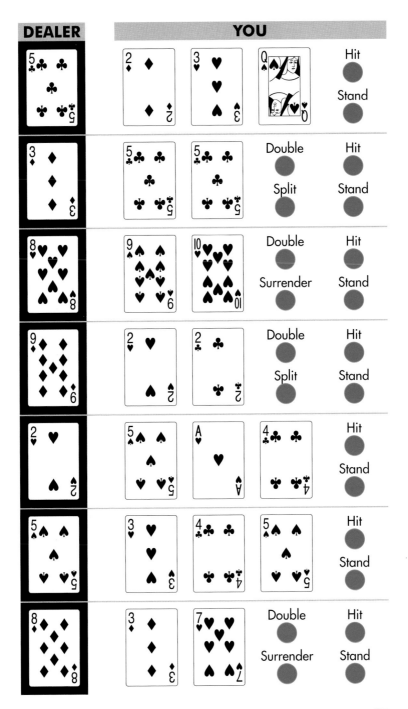

DEALER	YOU			
5♣	2♦	3♥	Q♠	Hit / Stand
3♦	5♣	5♣		Double / Hit / Split / Stand
8♥	9♠	10♥		Double / Hit / Surrender / Stand
9♦	2♥	2♣		Double / Hit / Split / Stand
2♥	5♠	A♥	4♣	Hit / Stand
5♠	3♥	4♣	5♠	Hit / Stand
8♦	3♦	7♥		Double / Hit / Surrender / Stand

25

DEALER	YOU			

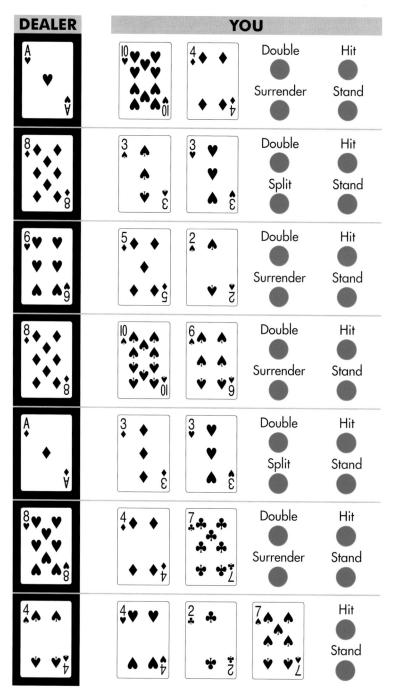

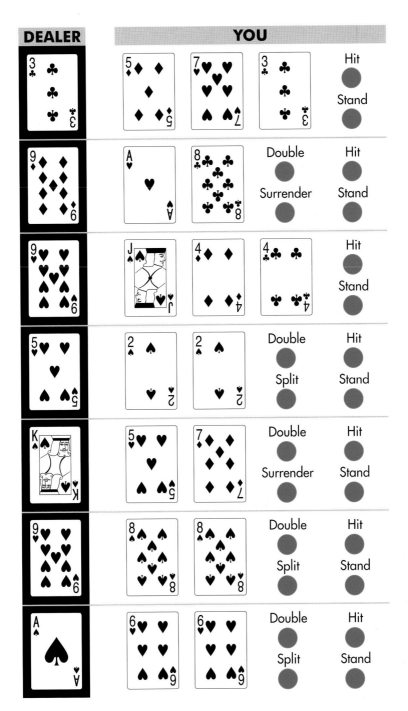

DEALER	YOU			
3♣	5♦	7♥	3♣	Hit / Stand
9♦	A♥	8♣	Double / Surrender	Hit / Stand
9♥	J♠	4♦	4♣	Hit / Stand
5♥	2♠	2♠	Double / Split	Hit / Stand
K♠	5♥	7♦	Double / Surrender	Hit / Stand
9♥	8♠	8♠	Double / Split	Hit / Stand
A♠	6♥	6♥	Double / Split	Hit / Stand

27

DEALER	YOU			

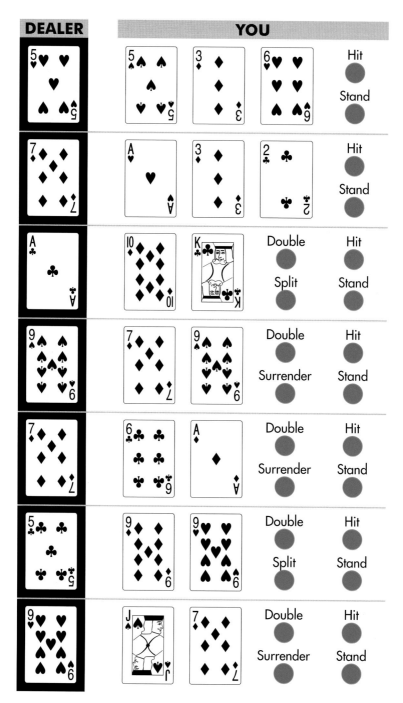

Row 1 — Dealer 5♥: You 5♠, 3♦, 6♥ — Hit / Stand

Row 2 — Dealer 7♦: You A♥, 3♦, 2♣ — Hit / Stand

Row 3 — Dealer A♣: You 10♦, K♣ — Double / Hit / Split / Stand

Row 4 — Dealer 9♠: You 7♦, 9♠ — Double / Hit / Surrender / Stand

Row 5 — Dealer 7♦: You 6♣, A♦ — Double / Hit / Surrender / Stand

Row 6 — Dealer 5♣: You 9♦, 9♥ — Double / Hit / Split / Stand

Row 7 — Dealer 9♥: You J♠, 7♦ — Double / Hit / Surrender / Stand

THE FOUR HORSEMEN

Whose Bright Idea Was Basic Strategy?

Stop me if you've heard this one: a Catholic, a Protestant, a Jew, and a black man join the army ... and create basic strategy. Never heard it? You're not alone. Only true blackjack aficionados are aware of the debt of gratitude owed to Roger Baldwin, Wilbert Cantey, Herbert Maisel, and James McDermott, collectively known as the "Four Horsemen of Aberdeen."

In the early 1950s, these four men served in the army at Aberdeen Proving Ground in Maryland. Using only pencils, paper, and clunky adding machines, they applied their considerable mathematical skills to the question of how best to play blackjack. The answer came in the form of an article titled "The Optimum Strategy in Blackjack" published in the September 1956 edition of the *Journal of the American Statistical Association*. (As of this writing, the article is available online at www.bjmath.com/bjmath/basic/cantey.pdf).

The strategy was nearly perfect, a remarkable achievement considering the resources available to the foursome. Edward O. Thorp drew on the research and analysis of the Four Horsemen for his 1962 bestseller *Beat the Dealer*, the book that popularized blackjack by introducing the world to basic strategy and card counting. Thorp had the benefit of MIT computers to refine the strategy and correct its few inaccuracies. Other blackjack analysts such as Julian Braun, Peter Griffin, and Stanford Wong then brought basic strategy to a pristine state of reliability and adapted it to various playing conditions and card-counting systems. Yet all these blackjack luminaries stand on the shoulders of four guys who never counted cards and never played blackjack for big money. In fact, the legendary Horsemen pretty much lost interest in blackjack after the early 1960s.

For their pioneering work, Baldwin, Cantey, Maisel, and McDermott finally got their due and were inducted into the Blackjack Hall of Fame in 2008. That's right, there's a Blackjack Hall of Fame; you can find it in the Barona Casino near San Diego. Odds are such a thing would never have existed if the Horsemen hadn't come along.

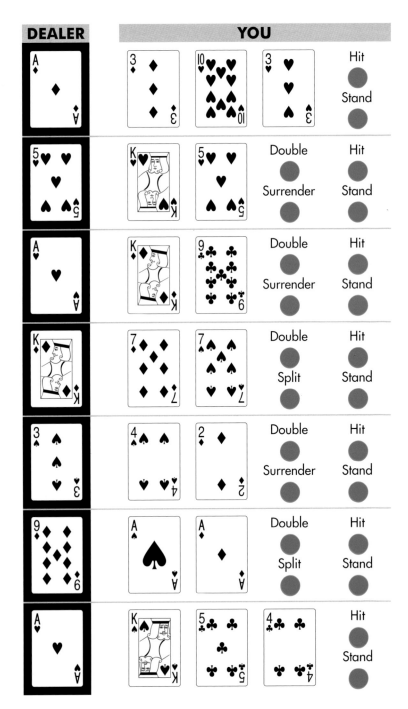

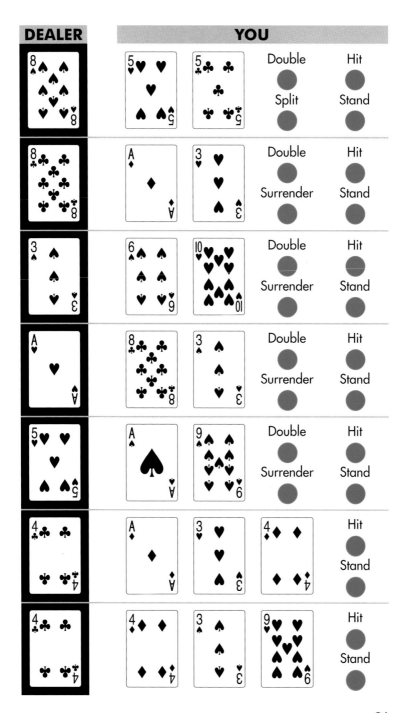

DEALER	YOU			
8♠	5♥	5♣	Double / Split	Hit / Stand
8♣	A♦	3♥	Double / Surrender	Hit / Stand
3♠	6♠	10♥	Double / Surrender	Hit / Stand
A♥	8♣	3♠	Double / Surrender	Hit / Stand
5♥	A♠	9♠	Double / Surrender	Hit / Stand
4♣	A♦	3♥	4♦	Hit / Stand
4♣	4♦	3♠	9♥	Hit / Stand

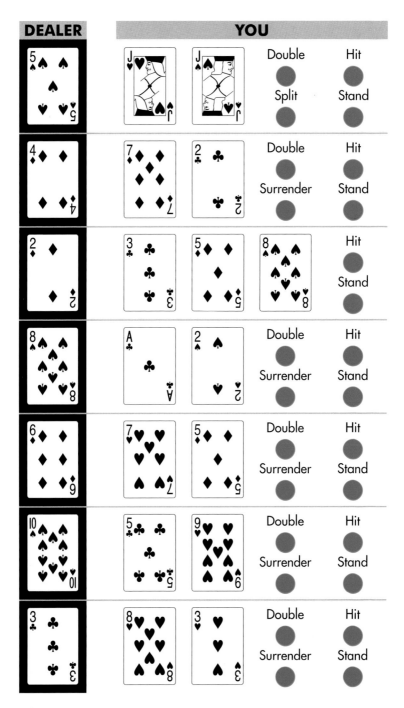

DEALER	YOU			
5♠	J♥	J♠	Double Hit	Split Stand
4♦	7♦	2♣	Double Hit	Surrender Stand
2♦	3♣	5♦	8♠	Hit Stand
8♠	A♣	2♠	Double Hit	Surrender Stand
6♦	7♥	5♦	Double Hit	Surrender Stand
10♠	5♣	9♥	Double Hit	Surrender Stand
3♣	8♥	3♥	Double Hit	Surrender Stand

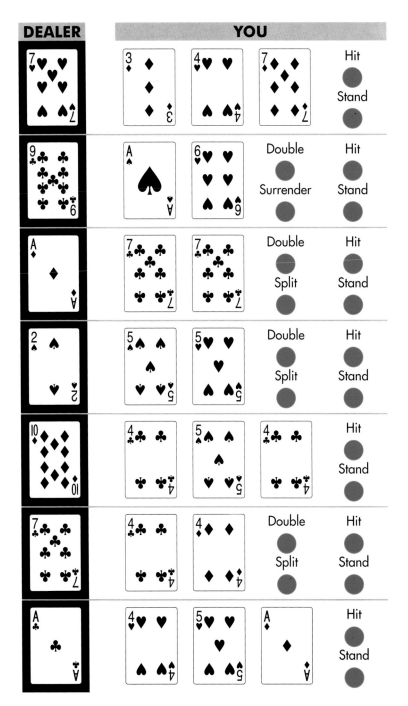

HOUSE RULES AND
THE HOUSE ADVANTAGE

Variations in blackjack rules will not only alter your basic strategy, they will also change the house edge. The number of decks used in a game is only one variable. Scouting out the different games you'll find subtle and less-than-subtle differences in the playing conditions. Any change has some effect—large or small, positive or negative—on the player's expectation.

The charts on page 35 will help you determine the value of a blackjack game. They show you the effect of various playing conditions on your expectation. Rules that increase your expectation (in other words, reduce the house edge) have a plus sign. Rules that decrease your expectation (in other words, increase the house edge) have a minus sign. These percentages will vary slightly because the effects change based on the number of decks in play. Still, the charts give you a good idea of what to look for (and look out for).

We'll use the old-time Las Vegas Strip rules as our baseline:

- Single deck
- Dealer stands on soft 17
- Double down on any two cards
- No doubling after splitting pairs
- Pairs can be split up to four times (except aces)
- Split aces get only one card
- No surrender

Assuming the use of proper basic strategy, the house edge in the old-time Strip game is near zero. (That's why it's all but gone the way of the dinosaurs and the dodos.) With this essentially even game as our baseline, we can then add and subtract the various effects shown on the next page to see what we're up against in any particular game. Keep in mind that the expectation is contingent on using the proper basic strategy for the particular rules.

HOUSE-FAVORABLE RULE VARIATIONS

Rule	Effect on Player Expectation
Two decks	−0.32%
Four decks	−0.48%
Six decks	−0.54%
Eight decks	−0.58%
Dealer hits soft 17	−0.20%
Double down only on 11 (no soft, no 10, no 9, no 8)	−0.78%
Double down only on 10 or 11 (no soft, no 9, no 8)	−0.26%
Double down only on 9, 10, 11 (no soft, no 8)	−0.14%
No resplitting of any pairs	−0.03%
Blackjack pays 6 to 5	−1.39%
Blackjack pays 1 to 1	−2.32%

PLAYER-FAVORABLE RULE VARIATIONS

Rule	Effect on Player Expectation
Blackjack pays 2 to 1	+2.32%
Double down on any number of cards	+0.24%
Double down after splitting pairs	+0.14%
Late surrender	+0.06%
Early surrender	+0.62%
Six-card winner	+0.15%
Player's 21 pushes dealer's 10-up blackjack	+0.16%
Resplitting of aces	+0.06%
Draw to split aces	+0.14%

There's so much variety in blackjack offerings, you can't afford not to comparison shop. I'm not even talking about scoping out a whole geographic region—you'll sometimes find variations of over half a percent in the same casino. If the rules aren't clearly posted at a table, make sure to ask. Good games may be hidden among bad games and vice versa.

Unfortunately, the most favorable rules are often found at tables that require a high minimum bet. Don't play above your head just to gain a few tenths of a percentage in advantage. At higher stakes, your bankroll can fluctuate wildly and disappear quickly. Plus, no matter how great a game you find, you'll still be playing at an overall disadvantage.

OMINOUS TRENDS

Consider this a PSA for all blackjack players. There are two trends in blackjack rules that players must hold the line against.

The Soft 17 Contagion

The dealer hitting soft 17 has become increasingly ubiquitous. This rule has long been the standard in low-stakes one- and two-deck games, which is tolerable because it's the casino's way of offsetting the player's advantage of playing with fewer decks. But now one finds this rule infiltrating six- and eight-deck games. There's no excuse for that; the casinos have decided to slip in an extra advantage on uninformed or apathetic players. Read the table felt to see the rule. If you're playing a multiple-deck game and the dealer hits soft 17, try to take your money elsewhere. The same rules—except the dealer stands on soft 17—may be at a table five feet away or at the casino next door.

The 6–5 Rip-Off

However irritating the soft-17 situation is, it's nothing compared to the alarming number of blackjack games that pay only 6 to 5 on a natural (slang for a blackjack). The casinos, devious and greedy creatures that they are, have tacked on this lousy payout to most single-deck games. The casinos know most players have a sense that playing a single deck is a "smart bet," but many players don't know how bad a 6–5 payout is. In the world of blackjack, it's larcenous—a 1.39% jump in house edge. This alteration alone balloons the house edge anywhere from three to six times beyond what you'd expect. I don't even consider a table that pays 6–5 on a natural to be a legitimate game of blackjack. Walk away from any table that offers less than 3–2 on blackjack. Let's try to eliminate this blackjack blight before it spreads any further. (For the benefits of proper-pay blackjack, see "Super Natural" on page 60.)

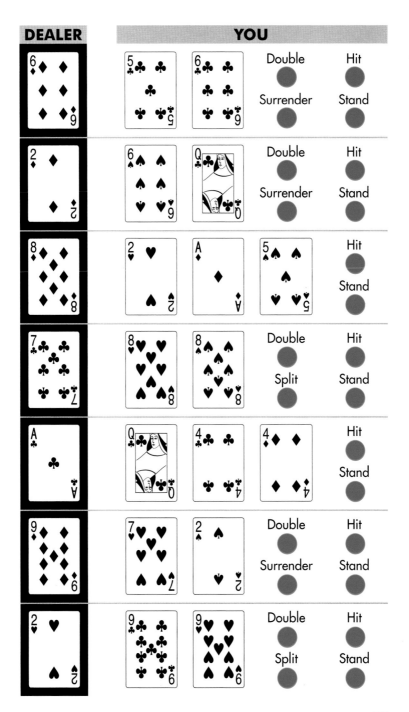

37

DEALER	YOU			

Dealer 6♥ — You: A♥, 3♥ — Double, Hit, Surrender, Stand

Dealer 9♣ — You: 8♠, 5♣, 4♦ — Hit, Stand

Dealer 5♠ — You: 6♠, 7♠ — Double, Hit, Surrender, Stand

Dealer 5♦ — You: 2♠, 3♥, A♠ — Hit, Stand

Dealer 9♣ — You: A♣, 9♥ — Double, Hit, Surrender, Stand

Dealer 3♦ — You: 7♥, Q♦ — Double, Hit, Surrender, Stand

Dealer 2♣ — You: 7♥, 2♣, 3♣ — Hit, Stand

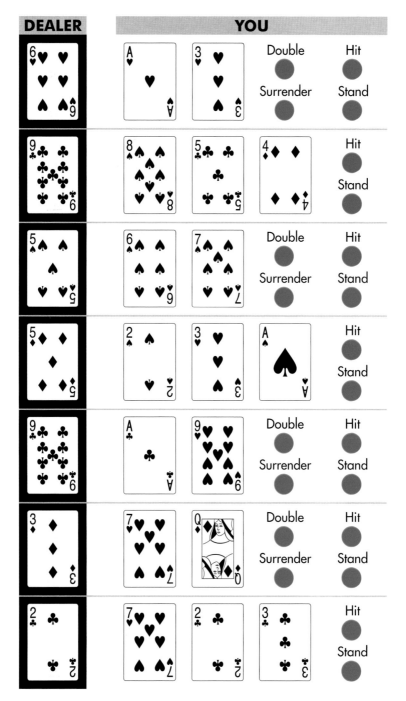

38

DEALER	YOU			
8♦	6♠	A♣	Double Hit	Surrender Stand
5♣	3♥	7♠	Double Hit	Surrender Stand
3♦	3♣	10♥	Double Hit	Surrender Stand
3♦	2♥	A♦	Double Hit	Surrender Stand
6♠	9♥	5♣	Double Hit	Surrender Stand
A♦	A♠	8♦	Double Hit	Surrender Stand
Q♥	4♥	7♠	Double Hit	Surrender Stand

39

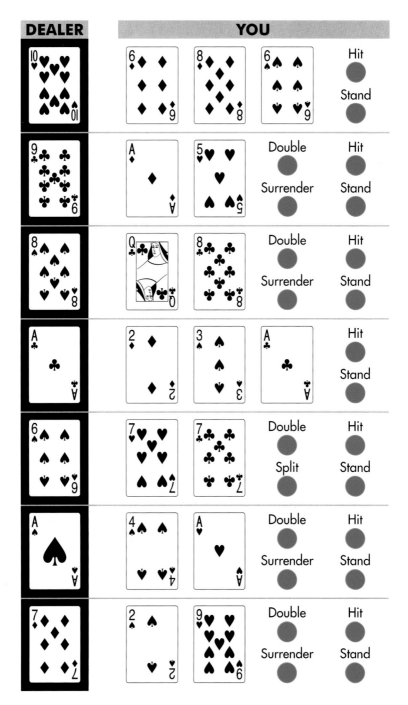

DEALER	YOU				
10♥	6♦	8♦	6♠	Hit ●	
				Stand ●	
9♣	A♦	5♥	Double ●	Hit ●	
			Surrender ●	Stand ●	
8♠	Q♣	8♣	Double ●	Hit ●	
			Surrender ●	Stand ●	
A♣	2♦	3♠	A♣	Hit ●	
				Stand ●	
6♠	7♥	7♣	Double ●	Hit ●	
			Split ●	Stand ●	
A♠	4♠	A♥	Double ●	Hit ●	
			Surrender ●	Stand ●	
7♦	2♠	9♥	Double ●	Hit ●	
			Surrender ●	Stand ●	

40

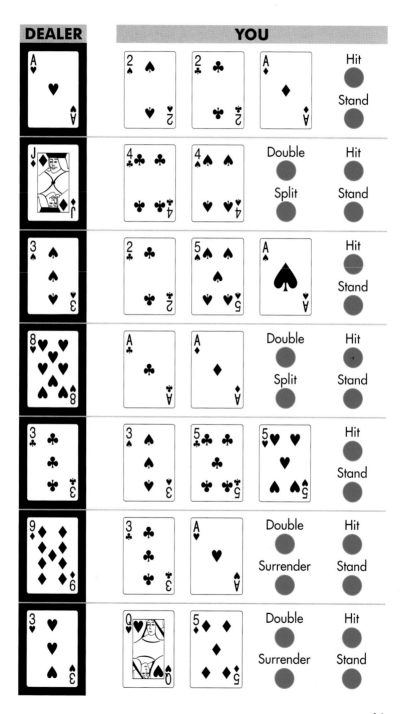

DEALER	YOU			
A♥	2♠	2♣	A♦	Hit / Stand
J♦	4♣	4♠	Double / Split	Hit / Stand
3♠	2♣	5♠	A♠	Hit / Stand
8♥	A♣	A♦	Double / Split	Hit / Stand
3♣	3♠	5♣	5♥	Hit / Stand
9♦	3♣	A♥	Double / Surrender	Hit / Stand
3♥	Q♥	5♦	Double / Surrender	Hit / Stand

41

SINGLE DECK VS. MULTIPLE DECK

The main quiz of this book assumes that you're playing a multiple-deck game because that's what's most commonly offered. However, *all else being equal*, you would prefer to play in a game with fewer decks. A single-deck game has nearly a 0.6% advantage over its eight-deck counterpart, and a 0.3% edge over a double-deck offering. These are significant amounts in the battle for advantage. (Thankfully, the damage levels off as decks increase. There's not a huge difference between playing six decks or eight decks.)

But why should the number of decks make a difference? At first blush, it doesn't seem logical. It even seems anti-mathematical. After all, the playing cards occur in the same proportion in every deck—why should it matter if you use one deck or a hundred? The answer is that the effect of removing cards is much larger in single-deck games, and more beneficial to the player. Let's take a look at the different ways multiple decks erode our advantage.

• The player gets fewer blackjacks in a multiple-deck game. As we already discussed, blackjacks are very valuable because they pay us 3 to 2. We'll see (on page 60) how a natural will, on average, occur once every 20.7 hands in a single-deck game. We can apply the same method to determine the likelihood of blackjack in a six-deck game:

$$(^{24}\!/_{312} \times {}^{96}\!/_{311}) + (^{96}\!/_{312} \times {}^{24}\!/_{311}) = 0.04749 = 4.75\%$$

Now we can expect to receive a blackjack only once every 21.1 hands. It's a small difference, but it adds up over time.

• While the chance of getting a blackjack decreases with more decks, the chance of the dealer getting a blackjack when you do *increases*. Why? Because the effect of removing your blackjack cards is greater in a single deck. In a single-deck game, the dealer duplicates our blackjack once in every 27.2 of our blackjack hands. With eight decks, we find that it's once in every 21.9 blackjack hands that we'll be deflated by a dealer duplication.

• The offensive maneuver of doubling down at the right times is also hurt by multiple decks. Let's say you have a hand of 11 composed of the 3♦ and the 8♣. The dealer is showing the 6♠

as her upcard. (Suits are, of course, irrelevant in blackjack—you'll see why I included them in a moment.) As basic strategy dictates, you double down. What are your chances of receiving your ideal 10-value card?

Let's look at two scenarios: the one-deck game vs. the six-deck game. In both cases, we're working only with the knowledge of three cards removed from the deck. So the single-deck game has 49 unknown cards left and the six-deck game has 309 unknown cards left. The probability of receiving a 10-value card works out as follows:

Single-deck game: $^{16}\!/_{49}$ = 32.65%
Six-deck game: $^{96}\!/_{309}$ = 31.07%

So we have less of a chance to get our dream card in the six-deck game. Why is that? The number of 10-value cards is proportional, so it's not their fault. The problem is the multiples of the cards you've already seen. In a single-deck game, the 3♦, 8♣, and 6♠ are gone for good. But in a six-deck game, each of those particular cards has five "clones" living on in the pack. That means there are 15 extra cards that hurt your chances of getting a 10-value card. If we got rid of those 15 cards, our chances of getting a 10 would be $^{96}\!/_{294}$ = 32.65%. That, of course, is same 32.65% chance that occurs with a single deck. Now you have a vivid example of why multiple decks dilute the impact of individual cards being removed—and why doubling down loses some of its oomph when more decks are in play.

• In a multiple-deck game, the dealer busts less frequently. The dealer has more ways to avoid busting when there are more small cards available. This reduction in busts helps the dealer more than the player because the house rules force the dealer to hit more often than the player does.

Sadly, this conversation is mostly moot. It's extremely difficult these days to find a single-deck game that hasn't been saddled with the awful 6–5 payout on blackjack. *Never play a single-deck game that pays 6–5 on blackjack!* The casinos are looking for suckers who will become loyal to this lousy form of blackjack. You're much better off with the big shoes with the better rules.

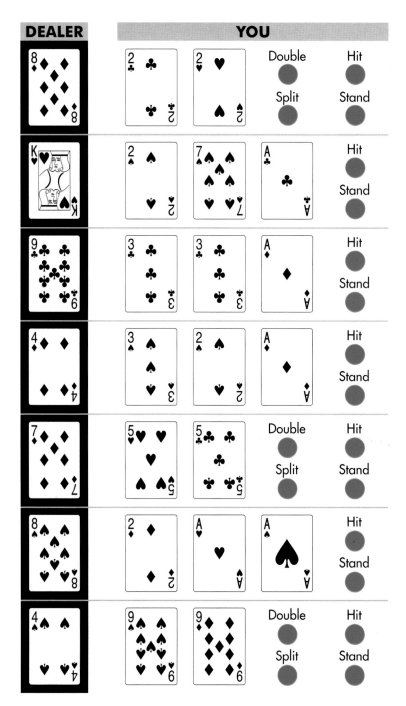

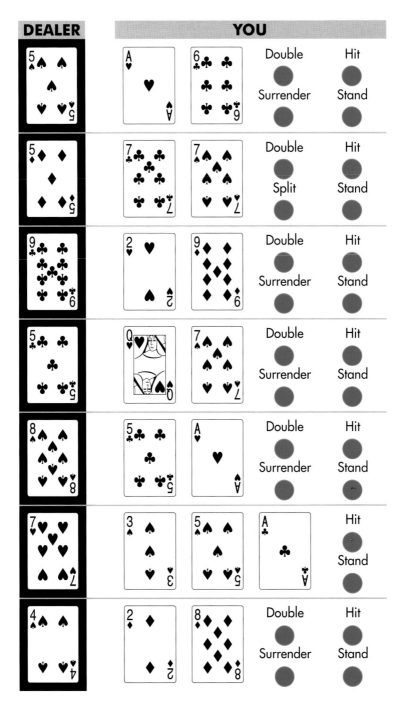

DEALER	YOU			
5♠	A♥	6♣	Double / Hit / Surrender / Stand	
5♦	7♣	7♠	Double / Hit / Split / Stand	
9♣	2♥	9♦	Double / Hit / Surrender / Stand	
5♣	Q♥	7♠	Double / Hit / Surrender / Stand	
8♠	5♣	A♥	Double / Hit / Surrender / Stand	
7♥	3♠	5♠	A♣	Hit / Stand
4♠	2♦	8♦	Double / Hit / Surrender / Stand	

45

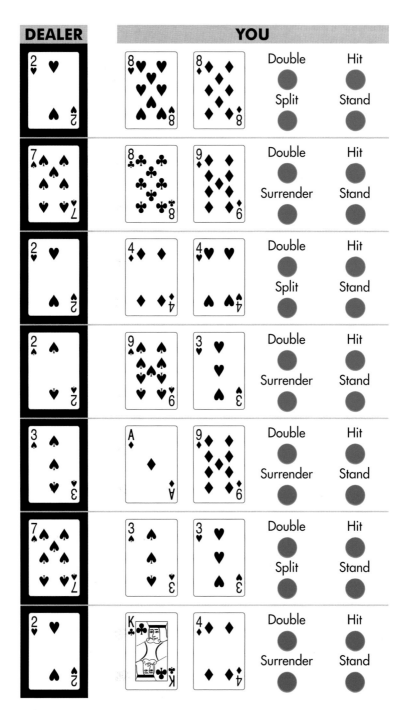

DEALER	YOU			
2♥	8♥ 8♦	Double	Hit	
		Split	Stand	
7♠	8♣ 9♦	Double	Hit	
		Surrender	Stand	
2♥	4♦ 4♥	Double	Hit	
		Split	Stand	
2♠	9♠ 3♥	Double	Hit	
		Surrender	Stand	
3♠	A♦ 9♦	Double	Hit	
		Surrender	Stand	
7♠	3♠ 3♥	Double	Hit	
		Split	Stand	
2♥	K♣ 4♦	Double	Hit	
		Surrender	Stand	

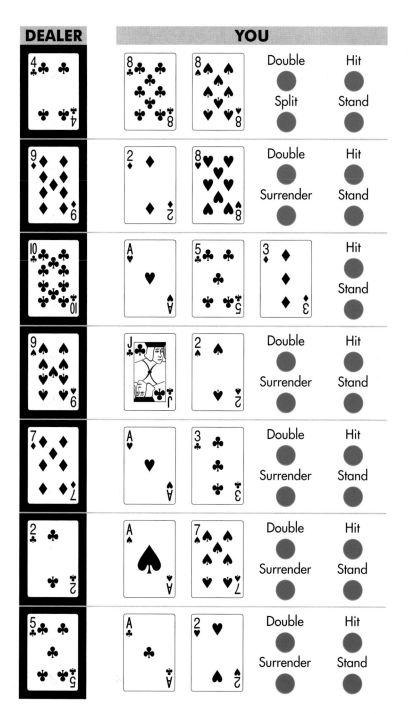

DEALER	YOU			
4♣	8♣	8♠	Double / Split	Hit / Stand
6♦	2♦	8♥	Double / Surrender	Hit / Stand
10♣	A♥	5♣	3♦	Hit / Stand
9♠	J♣	2♠	Double / Surrender	Hit / Stand
7♦	A♥	3♣	Double / Surrender	Hit / Stand
2♣	A♠	7♠	Double / Surrender	Hit / Stand
5♣	A♣	2♥	Double / Surrender	Hit / Stand

47

DEALER	YOU			
4♦	7♥	7♦	**Double** **Split**	**Hit** **Stand**
7♣	4♠	Q♦ 3♦		**Hit** **Stand**
2♠	6♥	6♣	**Double** **Split**	**Hit** **Stand**
2♦	A♣	3♥	**Double** **Surrender**	**Hit** **Stand**
A♠	9♦	A♦	**Double** **Surrender**	**Hit** **Stand**
6♠	A♥	5♠	**Double** **Surrender**	**Hit** **Stand**
K♠	6♥	6♥	**Double** **Split**	**Hit** **Stand**

48

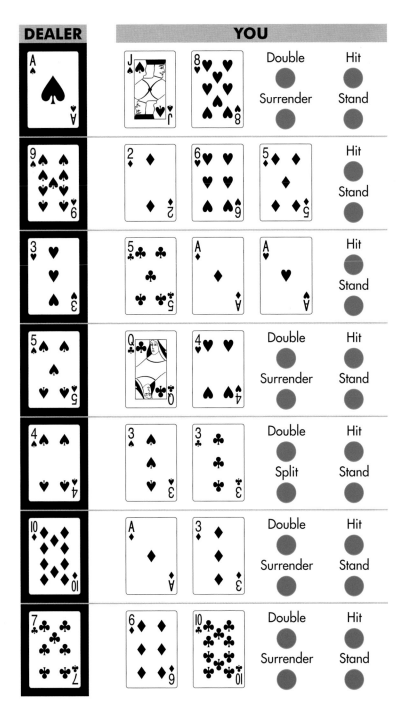

DEALER	YOU			
A♠	J♠	8♥	**Double** ● **Surrender** ●	**Hit** ● **Stand** ●
9♠	2♦	6♥	5♦	**Hit** ● **Stand** ●
3♥	5♣	A♦	A♥	**Hit** ● **Stand** ●
5♠	Q♣	4♥		**Double** ● **Surrender** ● **Hit** ● **Stand** ●
4♠	3♠	3♣		**Double** ● **Split** ● **Hit** ● **Stand** ●
10♦	A♦	3♦		**Double** ● **Surrender** ● **Hit** ● **Stand** ●
7♣	6♦	10♣		**Double** ● **Surrender** ● **Hit** ● **Stand** ●

49

THE DEAL WITH THE DEALER'S CARD

Why is the dealer's upcard so crucial? Because it's a gauge of the strength or weakness of the dealer's hand. This gives us insight into basic strategy: there are times when we let the dealer incur the risk and times when we must bear the risk ourselves. The chart below shows the probability of the dealer achieving certain hands based on his upcard. (Because the dealer must hit any hand lower than 17, he will always have a final hand of 17–21 or he will bust.)

		Final Hand					
		17	18	19	20	21	Bust
Upcard	2	14%	13%	13%	13%	12%	35%
	3	13%	13%	12%	12%	12%	38%
	4	13%	12%	12%	12%	11%	40%
	5	12%	12%	12%	10%	11%	43%
	6	17%	10%	11%	10%	10%	42%
	7	37%	14%	8%	8%	7%	26%
	8	13%	36%	13%	7%	7%	24%
	9	13%	10%	36%	12%	6%	23%
	10	12%	12%	12%	36%	4%	24%
	Ace	19%	19%	19%	18%	8%	17%

The dealer has a much higher probability of busting with upcards of 2 through 6 as compared to 7 through ace. You can see how this translates to decisions on the basic strategy chart. When the dealer has a weak card we let him take the chance of busting and we get more aggressive with doubles and splits. But when the dealer has 7 through ace, he has a good chance of reaching a pat hand (a hand of 17–21). Even with just a 7, the dealer will make a pat hand 74% of the time. That means he'll bust only one-quarter of the time. In that case, we hit our stiff hands (hands of 12–16), because it would be too risky to stand and hope the dealer will bust.

The chart also illustrates why the informal "rule of 10," which assumes that every unseen card is a 10, is a reasonable rule of thumb. Tens are by far the highest percentage cards in the deck, making up 30.8% (16⁄52) of a deck's composition. It's true that the next card may not be a 10 (in fact, most of the time it won't be), but it's often useful to assume it will be in order to make sense of basic strategy.

So when the dealer has a 7, lo and behold, he's most likely to end up with a pat hand of 17. In that case, we have to hit our stiff hands whether we like it or not. But when the dealer has a 6 up we think "ah, he probably has a total of 16" and expect he has a good chance of busting (a 42% chance as the chart shows). Therefore, against 6, we stand with our stiff hands (and our pat hands of course), and we double and split at most every opportunity.

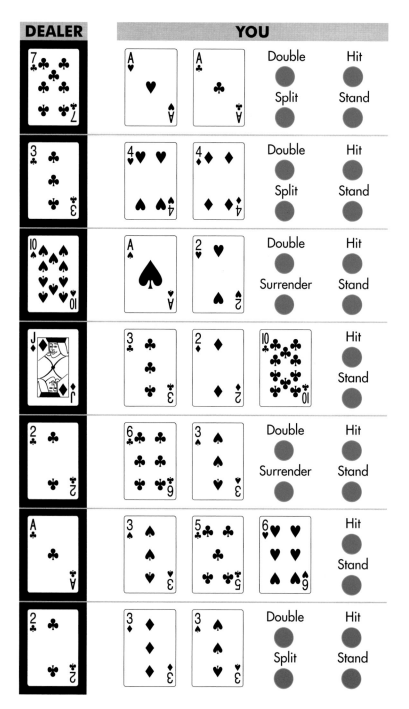

DEALER	YOU			
7♣	A♥	A♣	Double / Split	Hit / Stand
3♣	4♥	4♦	Double / Split	Hit / Stand
10♥	A♠	2♥	Double / Surrender	Hit / Stand
J♦	3♣	2♦	10♣	Hit / Stand
2♣	6♣	3♠	Double / Surrender	Hit / Stand
A♣	3♠	5♣	6♥	Hit / Stand
2♣	3♦	3♠	Double / Split	Hit / Stand

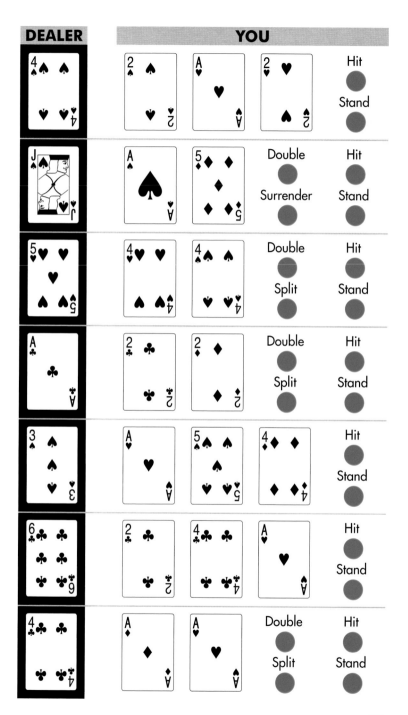

DEALER	YOU			
4♠	2♠	A♥	2♥	Hit / Stand
J♠	A♠	5♦		Double / Hit / Surrender / Stand
5♥	4♥	4♠		Double / Hit / Split / Stand
A♣	2♣	2♦		Double / Hit / Split / Stand
3♠	A♥	5♠	4♦	Hit / Stand
6♣	2♣	4♣	A♥	Hit / Stand
4♣	A♦	A♥		Double / Hit / Split / Stand

53

BASICALLY BAD STRATEGIES

You bought this book because you're a basic strategy believer. However, you may be curious about other "strategies" you come across. Here are some ill-advised approaches that possess the patina of logic but fall apart under closer scrutiny.

Do as the Dealer Does
With the mimic-the-dealer strategy, the player plays out his hand according to the dealer's hit and stand rules. It has a certain allure: you stay even with the dealer by doing what he does *and* you get paid 3 to 2 on blackjack. Time to break the bank! One big problem: when both the dealer and the player bust, the house wins. The dealer busts 28.2% of the time; a player mimicking the house will also bust 28.2% of the time. The player is hurt whenever there is a double bust, which will occur about 8% of the time (0.282 × 0.282). That leaves the player with an 8% disadvantage. The 2.3% payoff for naturals cuts into this house edge, but reduces it only to 5.7%. Therefore, imitation is an invitation to give away your bankroll.

No-Bust Strategy
Using the no-bust strategy, players refuse to take a card if they have any chance of busting. That means never hitting with a hard 12 or greater. Again, one can see the appeal. Intellectually, we know that much of the dealer's advantage comes from winning double busts (see above). Emotionally, it's very frustrating to hit your 13 against the dealer's 7, bust your hand, and then watch as the dealer proceeds to turn over a 9, add a 6, and bust his own hand.

However, players who don't hit their stiff hands against the dealer's strong cards of 7 through ace are playing a losing game. When the dealer has a 7 or higher showing, he will have a pat hand 74% of the time. That means we would win only one of four hands if we stood on a stiff hand—because our only hope is that the dealer will bust. By "staying in the game" with the no-bust strategy, you'll be giving up a house edge that's been estimated at somewhere between 5% and 8%. That will get you out of the game right fast.

BS vs. Basic Strategy

Either at the tables or on the Internet, you may make the acquaintance of the blackjack lunatic fringe. One conspiracy theory contends that basic strategy was created by the casinos to guarantee that players will lose. A variation of this is that basic strategy possesses an inherent flaw that only a few people know and they have conspired to cover it up. Others will try to convince you that basic strategy doesn't reflect real life because it's based on computer simulations. (Never mind that the computer simulations are perfectly suited to examining the real-life effects of different decisions over an enormous number of hands.)

There will be those who will tell you that you just have to be aware of hot and cold streaks and "how the cards are running." They don't advocate that you actually count cards, which is a legitimate way to assess whether the remaining cards favor you or the dealer. No, instead you have to rely on some psychic sense or some deep connection to the elder gods or a "foolproof" system that will only cost you x number of dollars at a website.

Don't go down the rabbit hole: avoid the hazy thinking of the pontificators, crackpots, and hucksters. Independent mathematicians and analysts have shown time and time again that basic strategy is the way to go.

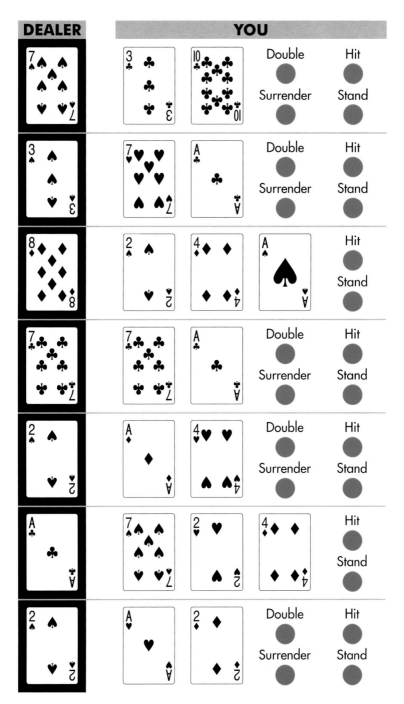

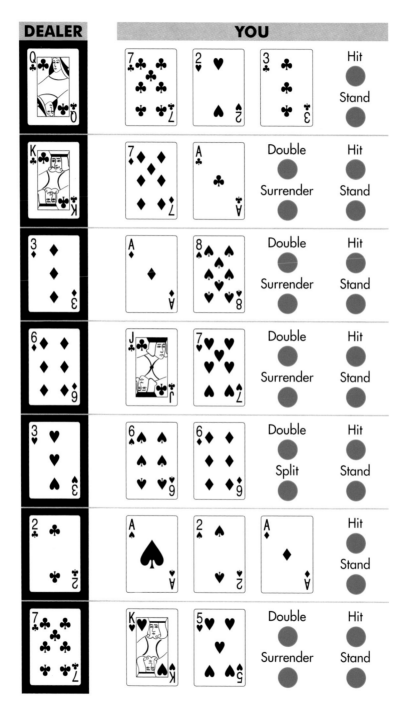

DEALER	YOU			
Q♣	7♣	2♥	3♣	Hit / Stand
K♣	7♦	A♣		Double / Hit / Surrender / Stand
3♦	A♦	8♠		Double / Hit / Surrender / Stand
6♦	J♣	7♥		Double / Hit / Surrender / Stand
3♥	6♠	6♦		Double / Hit / Split / Stand
2♣	A♠	2♠	A♦	Hit / Stand
7♣	K♥	5♥		Double / Hit / Surrender / Stand

57

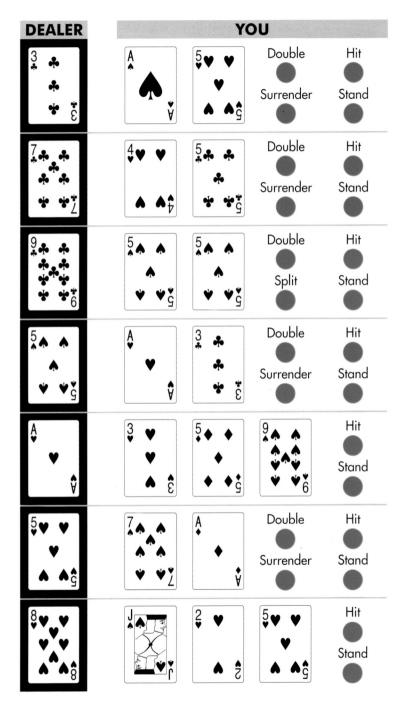

DEALER	YOU			
3 ♣	A ♠	5 ♥	Double · Hit · Surrender · Stand	
7 ♣	4 ♥	5 ♣	Double · Hit · Surrender · Stand	
9 ♣	5 ♠	5 ♠	Double · Hit · Split · Stand	
5 ♠	A ♥	3 ♣	Double · Hit · Surrender · Stand	
A ♥	3 ♥	5 ♦	9 ♠	Hit · Stand
5 ♥	7 ♠	A ♦	Double · Hit · Surrender · Stand	
8 ♥	J ♠	2 ♥	5 ♥	Hit · Stand

58

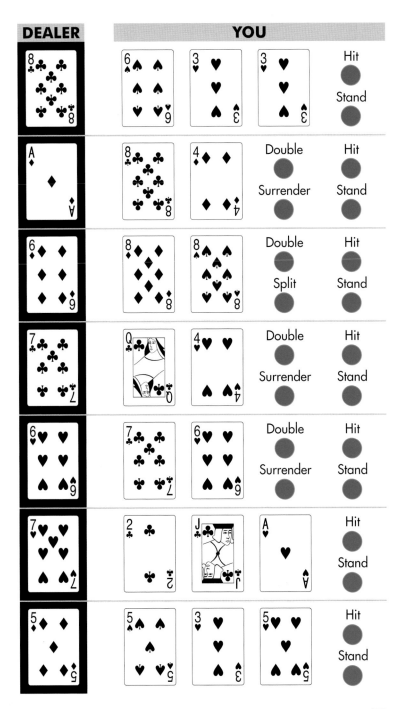

SUPER NATURAL

Alas, you won't find any blackjacks among the hands dealt in the IQ test because that would merely test your ability to grin, nod approvingly, or subtly pump your fist. But that doesn't mean we shouldn't sing the praises of receiving a blackjack.

Blackjack's payoff of 3 to 2 is in large part what separates this game from the other money-draining beasts in the casino. Let's discover just how valuable a blackjack is to the player's expectation.

Let's assume that you're playing the game in its pure (if not quite as prevalent) form: single-deck. What are your chances of getting a blackjack? To receive an ace as your first card, you have a chance of four (number of aces) out of 52 (total number of cards). To receive a 10-value card as your second card, you have a chance of 16 (number of 10-value cards in deck) out of 51 (total number of cards minus the first card you received). The probability of both these things happening is $4/52 \times 16/51$. But that's not the only way to receive a blackjack; you can also get a 10 as your first card ($16/52$) and then an ace as your second ($4/51$).

So our total probability of getting a blackjack dealt in a single deck is both of these possibilities added together:

$$(4/52 \times 16/51) + (16/52 \times 4/51) = 32/663 = 0.0483 = 4.83\%$$

Overall, you can expect to receive a blackjack 4.83% of the time, or once in every 20.7 hands. (That's an average: don't assume the dealer, the house, and the fates are cheating you if you don't see a blackjack in 50 or 100 hands.)

Now we must consider the cruel times when the dealer duplicates your blackjack and thus negates your 3-to-2 windfall. The chance of dealer having an ace is $3/50$ (your hand holds one ace and two cards from the deck), and his chance of then getting a 10 is $15/49$ (you have one 10 and three cards are gone from the deck). We also have to account for the reverse order: dealer gets a 10 ($15/50$) and then an ace ($3/49$). So we have the following:

$$(3/50 \times 15/49) + (15/50 \times 3/49) = 9/245 = 0.0367 = 3.67\%$$

Thus we have another tidbit to keep in mind for a single-deck game. When you have a blackjack, the dealer will rain on your parade 3.67% of the time, which is once in every 27.2 hands in which you have blackjack.

To calculate our "natural" advantage, we need to know how often the dealer *won't* duplicate a blackjack. So:

P(dealer doesn't have blackjack when we do) = 1 − 0.0367
$$= .9633$$
$$= 96.33\%$$

Now, we can see what the expected return is for our getting paid 3 to 2 on blackjack. Remember that the dealer has just as much of a chance to have blackjack as we do, but we don't have to pay the dealer 3 to 2. So here's how it breaks down:

Player advantage = [(player bj) × (no dealer bj) × (payoff)] +
$$[(\text{dealer bj}) \times (\text{no player bj}) \times (\text{payoff})]$$
$$= [(.0483) \times (.9633) \times (+1.5)] +$$
$$[(.0483) \times (.9633) \times (−1)]$$
$$= 0.0232$$
$$= 2.32\%$$

That 2.32% is a substantial part of why players have a fighting chance while playing blackjack.

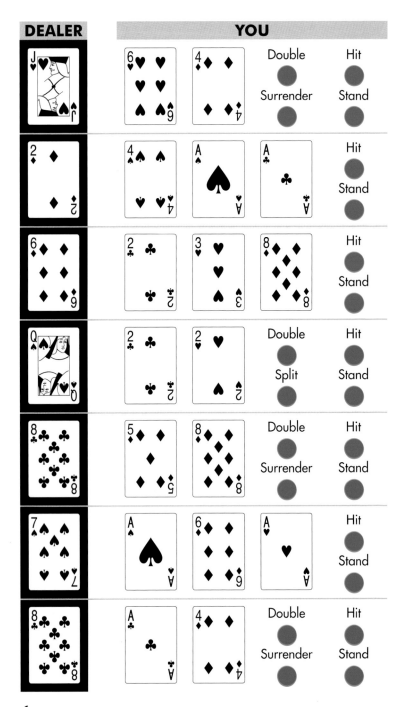

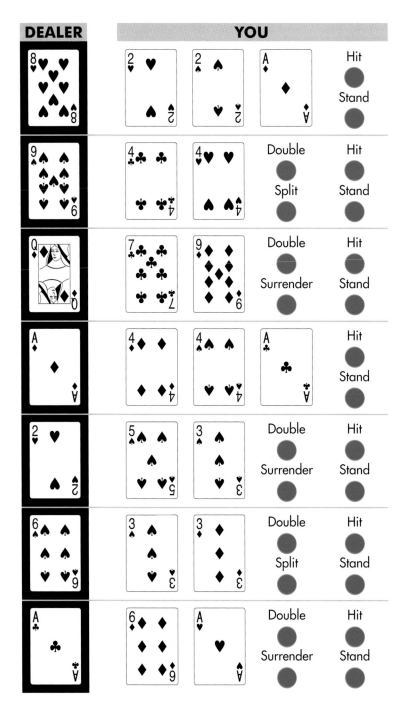

DEALER	YOU			
8♥	2♥	2♠	A♦	Hit / Stand
9♠	4♣	4♥		Double / Hit / Split / Stand
Q♦	7♣	9♦		Double / Hit / Surrender / Stand
A♦	4♦	4♠	A♣	Hit / Stand
2♥	5♠	3♠		Double / Hit / Surrender / Stand
6♠	3♠	3♦		Double / Hit / Split / Stand
A♣	6♦	A♥		Double / Hit / Surrender / Stand

63

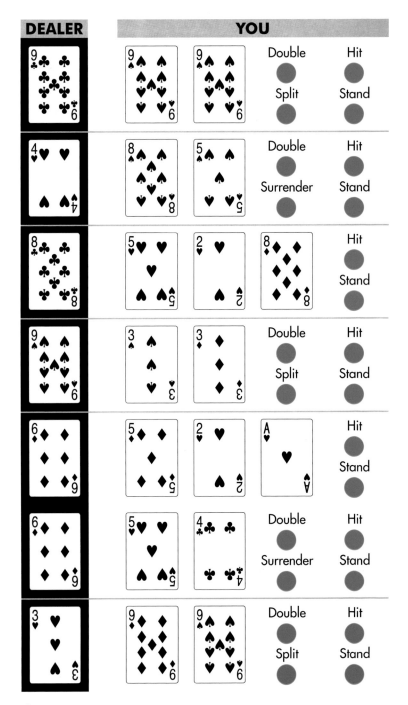

DEALER	YOU			

9♣ — **9♠** / **9♠** — Double · Hit · Split · Stand

4♥ — **8♠** / **5♠** — Double · Hit · Surrender · Stand

8♣ — **5♥** / **2♥** / **8♦** — Hit · Stand

9♠ — **3♠** / **3♦** — Double · Hit · Split · Stand

6♦ — **5♦** / **2♥** / **A♥** — Hit · Stand

6♦ — **5♥** / **4♣** — Double · Hit · Surrender · Stand

3♥ — **9♦** / **9♠** — Double · Hit · Split · Stand

64

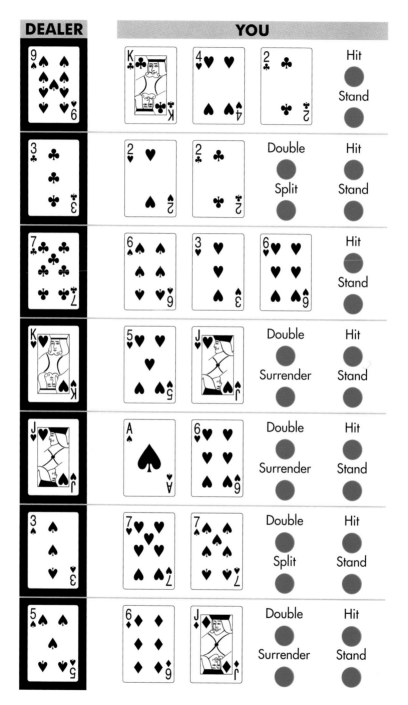

DEALER	YOU			
9♠	K♣	4♥	2♣	Hit / Stand
3♣	2♥	2♣	Double / Split	Hit / Stand
7♣	6♠	3♥	6♥	Hit / Stand
K♥	5♥	J♥	Double / Surrender	Hit / Stand
J♥	A♠	6♥	Double / Surrender	Hit / Stand
3♠	7♥	7♠	Double / Split	Hit / Stand
5♠	6♦	J♦	Double / Surrender	Hit / Stand

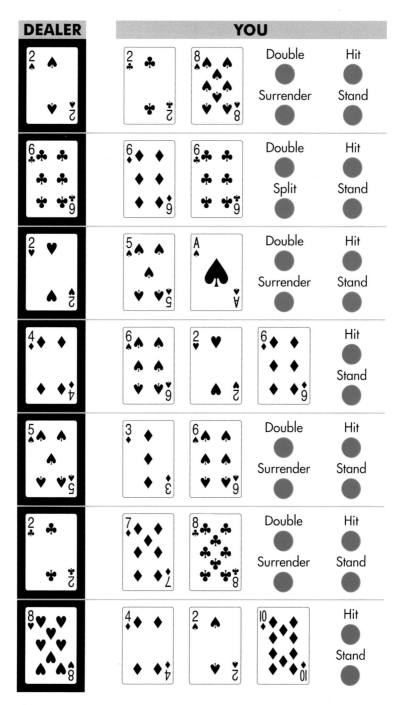

DEALER	YOU			
9♣	5♠	3♣	4♦	Hit Stand
8♦	7♣	2♦		Double Hit Surrender Stand
2♣	7♠	7♥		Double Hit Split Stand
6♦	4♠	2♥	9♠	Hit Stand
8♠	4♠	4♦		Double Hit Split Stand
4♥	7♣	9♦		Double Hit Surrender Stand
A♣	A♣	4♥	3♥	Hit Stand

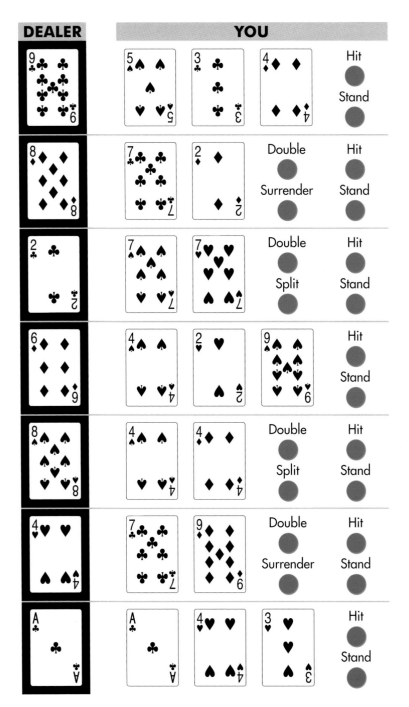

PEP TALK

Ya Gotta Believe

You know basic strategy is the right way to play. That's why you have this book. But sometimes even the most devout strategy player has his faith shaken. The happily inebriated player next to you stands with 14 against the dealer's ace and the dealer busts. The same guy then doesn't split his 8s against the dealer's 4 because he has a "bad feeling." Of course, his hunch gets "validated" as the dealer draws to a five-card 21.

Meanwhile, you're following basic strategy and every move turns out wrong. Your chips dwindle and Mr. Ignorance S. Bliss is raking it in. Worse yet, he clucks his tongue when you hit your 12 against the dealer's deuce—"I never do that"—and you bust.

You question what good basic strategy is doing you. You might as well get blitzed and use your latent psychic powers like this other guy. But you don't. You know that if there were ten thousand of your clones playing with ten thousand of his clones, your clones would come out way ahead. (And not just because you're so good-looking.) You know in the long run your moves will maximize every dollar you can get from the casino (barring card-counting). Still, the short run may not be kind to you. You may tap out your bankroll making all the right moves while the oblivious and intoxicated players outlast you with their head-scratching moves. Such is life. You have to accept that the proper play will pay off over time.

Consider this game. You can bet one dollar on the flip of coin. If you bet on heads and the coin comes up heads you win one dollar. If you bet on tails and the coin comes up tails you win 95 cents. Would you ever bet on tails? I hope not. You may be stymied by the devil-may-care gambler who correctly bets tails five times in a row. You may be losing money in the short run. But you would be foolish to take the worse bet—make the wrong move—because you don't like the short-term results.

Bet heads every time and you will come out ahead of anyone who messes around with the tails bet. It might take some time but it will happen. (Of course, you'll only be even with the house in this incredibly boring game.)

It may not seem as clear-cut and obvious in blackjack, but it is. The basic strategy chart is what makes it clear-cut and obvious. If you deviate from basic strategy, you'll be giving money away to the casino over the long run. I'd rather see that money in your pocket. Wouldn't you?

You must realize that basic strategy does not negate luck (or short-term fluctuations, as the mathematicians would call it). Do I know what will happen in one night of play? No. You may see your bankroll dwindle as you play perfectly, while the guy who doubles on 12 and stands on all 16s makes a fortune. That's the random nature of the cards. It won't last forever. Luck will yield to statistics over time.

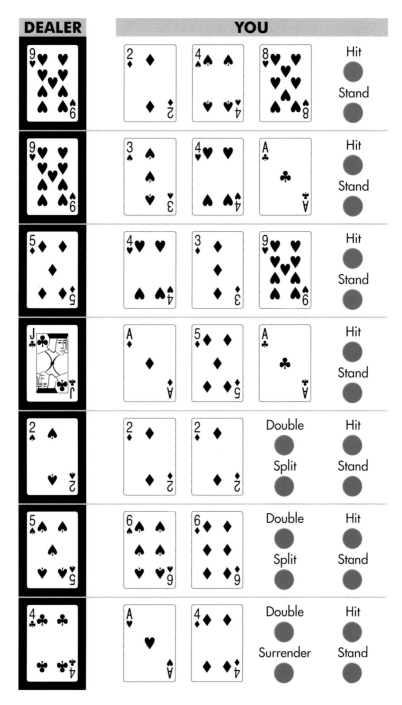

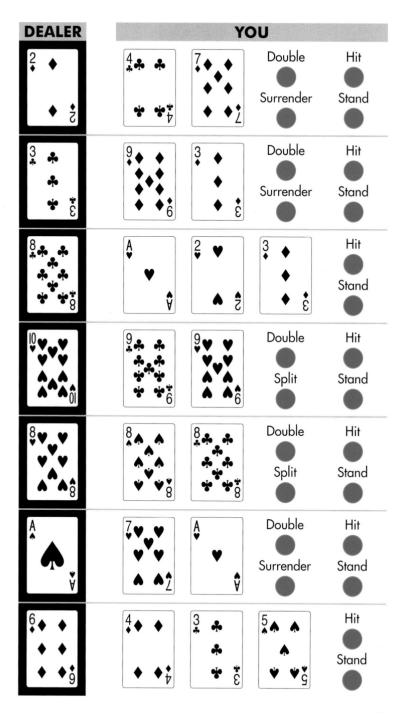

DEALER	YOU			
2♦	4♣	7♦	Double · Hit	Surrender · Stand
3♣	9♦	3♦	Double · Hit	Surrender · Stand
8♣	A♥	2♥	3♦	Hit · Stand
10♥	9♣	9♥	Double · Hit	Split · Stand
8♥	8♠	8♣	Double · Hit	Split · Stand
A♠	7♥	A♥	Double · Hit	Surrender · Stand
6♦	4♦	3♣	5♠	Hit · Stand

71

DEALER	YOU			
2♦	4♣	A♦	3♣	Hit / Stand
10♥	5♠	5♦	Double / Split	Hit / Stand
3♦	3♣	2♠	9♥	Hit / Stand
4♣	3♠	A♦	Double / Surrender	Hit / Stand
Q♣	A♥	A♠	Double / Split	Hit / Stand
5♣	3♠	9♠	Double / Surrender	Hit / Stand
J♠	8♦	8♠	Double / Split	Hit / Stand

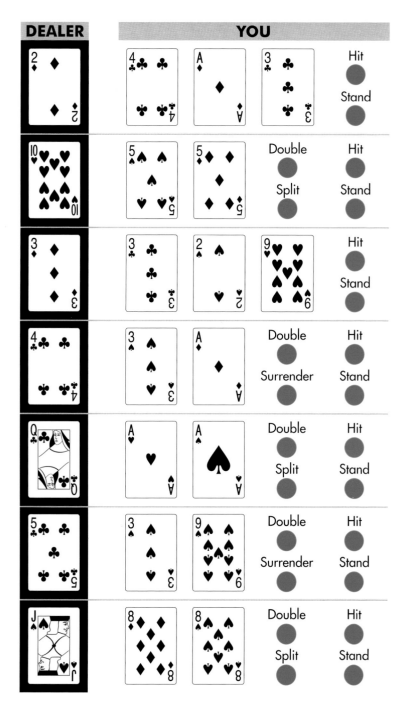

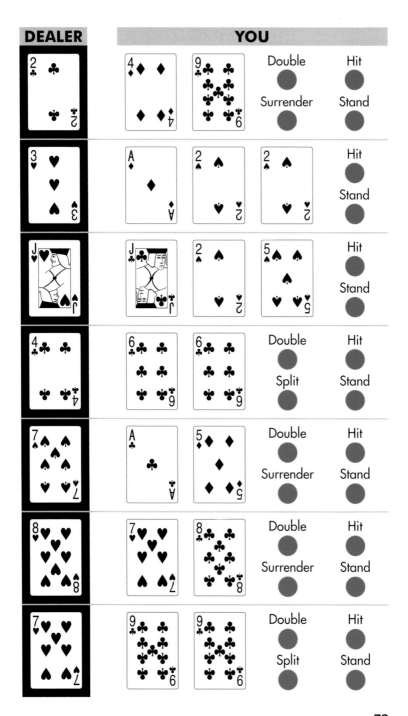

DEALER	YOU			
2 ♣	4 ♦	9 ♣	Double / Surrender	Hit / Stand
3 ♥	A ♦	2 ♠	2 ♠	Hit / Stand
J ♥	J ♣	2 ♠	5 ♠	Hit / Stand
4 ♣	6 ♣	6 ♣	Double / Split	Hit / Stand
7 ♠	A ♣	5 ♦	Double / Surrender	Hit / Stand
8 ♥	7 ♥	8 ♣	Double / Surrender	Hit / Stand
7 ♥	9 ♣	9 ♣	Double / Split	Hit / Stand

73

BASIC STRATEGY: INSIDE THE NUMBERS

The logic of the basic strategy chart mostly plays out in a common-sense fashion. However, you may not be able to reason out every basic strategy move—some things you just have to take on mathematical faith. Let's examine some basic strategy decisions and look at the math behind the right moves. (The expected values are based on data provided at the Wizard of Odds website. The numbers are based on a six-deck game where the dealer stands on soft 17 and you can double after splitting.)

Stiff Hands

No one likes hitting their stiff hands (12–16) and facing the possibility of busting. But in blackjack you sometimes have to settle for the lesser of evils; in other words, the best decision is the best only because all the other ones are worse. Yes, we lose money when we hit a stiff hand, but sometimes we lose *less* than if we stood. For example:

16 vs. 7: Some players don't hit here, perhaps hoping that the dealer won't have a 10 underneath and will bust. Unfortunately, the dealer will bust only 26% of the time. We must chase him. On average, standing will cost us about $48 of every $100 we bet in this situation. Hitting will cost "only" $41 per $100. The hit decision saves us $7.

12 vs. 2 or 3: These are the only two exceptions to the common-sense approach of never hitting a stiff when the dealer has a weak card. You can't assume that the dealer will have a 10 underneath and then get another 10 to bust. Enough non-10 cards can benefit the dealer's 2 (or 3) as well as your 12 to make this hand worth hitting. When you stand against a deuce, you'll lose $29.33 of every $100 bet in that situation. When you hit you'll lose only $25.30. So you save $4.03 per $100. Against a dealer 3, hitting will save you about $1.97.

Doubling Down

When you double down, you're pressing your advantage against the house. But you have to do it at the appropriate times as indicated in basic strategy. That's how you'll increase your profits in the long run.

11 vs. 10: Don't wimp out by not doubling down here. Yes, the dealer has a big card, but so do you. Sure, you'll make $11.78 per $100 when you hit, but you'll turn that into $17.69 when you double down.

9 vs. 8: Home-brewed logic can lead to an ill-advised double-down in this situation. Some players misapply the "rule of 10" here (again, it's only a rough guide) and figure they should press the advantage of their theoretical 19 versus the dealer's theoretical 18. This thinking is further bolstered by the fact that you double your ace versus dealer's 10 and your 10 versus dealer's 9; a 9-versus-8 double seems like the next logical step. The numbers say otherwise. Hitting will lead to a $10.03 gain per $100 while doubling down will actually *cost* you an average of $2.12.

9 vs. 2: Okay, but you double 9 versus dealer's 3, 4, 5, and 6. Surely you double against 2. It's a very close call but the numbers say you don't. An expected return of $7.72 per $100 when hitting gets nudged down to $7.00 when doubling. (In a single-deck game, you would double.)

Splitting

There are three reasons why we split cards: we do it to win more, to lose less, and, best of all, to turn a loss into a win. A quick perusal of the strategy charts will bring some non-shocking news: we're aggressive with our splitting when the dealer has a weak card, especially 5 or 6. Even among those splits, some are defensive in nature (lose less) while others are offensive (win more).

Never split 10s ... not even against a 5 or 6. Some players are tempted to split 10s against a weak dealer card like a 6. It almost seems sensible: start with a 10 and exploit the dealer's vulnerability. But, in this case, greed, for lack of a better word, is bad. Standing on 20 versus 6 will make you a hefty $70.28 profit per $100 bet. The split will double your risk and drop your earnings down to $44.49. The numbers only get worse against other dealer upcards.

Always split 8s. Why always split 8s? Against a strong dealer upcard, it may seem like we're throwing good money after bad. Although we can often provide a common-sense rationale for splitting, in this case we have to defer to the all-knowing computer.

8–8 vs. ace: Do we really want to create two hands to take on an ace? Surprisingly, yes. We know 16 is a lousy start; playing this hand as a 16 we'd expect to lose $51.36 lost for every $100 bet. Playing it as two hands of 8 we'd expect to lose about $18.22 on each hand. Multiplied by two (for our two hands) we get a net loss of $36.44 of the original bet. So we end up saving $14.92.

8–8 vs. 7: Here's a hand that goes from pitiful to profitable. Hit the 8s and you stand to lose $40.84. Split the 8s and they may plump up nicely with a 10 or ace. Or you may have the opportunity to double if you receive a 2 or 3. Suddenly, you're in the black with an average profit of $31.89. That's a $72.73 about-face.

4–4 vs. 6: Dealers and other players may share this little nugget with you: Never split anything that starts with "f" (fours, fives, and faces). It's too bad that such a handy mnemonic isn't entirely true. In a multiple-deck game where you can double after splitting, you should split 4s against the dealer's 5 and 6. You may get a 6 or 7, and thus get more money on the table with a double. Just hitting the 4s against a 6 will earn $12.44 per $100 bet while splitting brings $16.82. Just remember to fine-tune the "f" rule and you'll fare fine.

9–9 vs. 7: Basic strategy sometimes throws in a monkey wrench. You're cruising along the row of 9–9 basic strategy decisions and the general impression is that you split on everything from 2 through 9. But wait—there's an exception. You actually stand against a 7. Relying on logic, we can see that our 18 should hold up well against the 7. Relying on statistics, we learn that we win $39.96 when standing as opposed to $36.42 when splitting.

Soft Hands

A lot of players have a hard time with soft hands. It's not that the hands are bad to get—they're quite good in general—but they cause hesitation and consternation. To maximize their value, you have to know when to double down because the ace's flexibility merits more aggressive play.

Soft 17 vs. 7: You *never* stand on soft 17. Some players are tempted to stand against a 7 because they think they'll wind up with a push. Standing is not an "even" play. You'll lose $10.38 for every $100 risked in this situation. But a hit will bring a long-term expected profit of $5.47. That's a swing of $15.85.

Soft 17 vs. 6: This calls for aggression. You don't just hit this soft 17, you double it. Standing (perish the thought) will get you $1.20, hitting $12.92, and doubling does its magic with a profit of $25.85.

Soft 18 vs. anything: Soft 18 has a unique status in multiple-deck basic strategy. It's the only hand that has three different correct decisions: you stand against 2, 7, and 8; you double down against 3–6; and you hit against 9, 10, and ace.

Soft 18 permits you to not be satisfied with a respectable value of 18. (A side note of interest: the average winning hand in blackjack is a little higher than 18.) You double down against 6, upgrading from a $28.04 win to $38.28. You're in trouble against a 9, but a hit will leave you with an average loss of $9.85 while standing will cost you $18.26. However, you stand against a 7. Your 18 should dominate the dealer's 7 and it does: you'll win $40.19 on average. Messing around with doubling down will drop your win to $22.37.

Surrender

Although surrender isn't available in every blackjack game, its proper application should be part of your basic strategy arsenal.

The surrender option permits you to "surrender" half your bet rather than playing out your hand. You'll need to ask if it is in effect when you sit down. If it is offered, it will most certainly be in the form of "late surrender," which means it is an option only after the dealer has checked for blackjack.

What's the reasoning for when to surrender? It's rather simple. Since you're giving up half your bet, you should surrender only in situations where your expectation is less than 50%. As you review the basic strategy charts, you'll see this doesn't happen as often as you think. For the IQ test's playing conditions, you surrender with a 16 against a dealer's 9, 10, and ace, and with a 15 against a dealer's 10.

If surrender is offered, don't hesitate to take advantage of it at the appropriate times. The play may occasionally elicit a snarky comment from a fellow player or even a dealer. More often you'll get curiosity and confusion from other players who aren't familiar with this unpublicized rule. Never you mind: save some money and fight again another hand.

Insurance Scam

The rule is simple for a player who does not count cards: ***Never take insurance.*** Insurance doesn't actually "insure" anything. It's merely a side bet about whether or not the dealer has a 10-value card in the hole when there's an ace showing.

Why is the side bet a bad proposition for basic strategy players? In order for insurance to be an even bet (with a correct payoff of 2 to 1) one in every three cards (33.3%) must be a 10. But, in fact, only 16 out of 52 cards (30.8%) are 10s—that's one in every 3.25 cards. The house edge on the insurance bet in a six-deck game is, on average, a whopping 7.4%.

What about taking even money when you have blackjack and the dealer has an ace? Don't do it. Dealers, fellow players, and casino kibitzers may tell you otherwise. They'll say you're crazy to turn down a guaranteed payoff. They're wrong.

First, realize that taking even money is exactly the same thing as insuring a blackjack. It's just a way of expediting the process rather than having you actually place the insurance bet.

Here's the expectation calculation for a $1 bet when you have a natural, the dealer has an ace, and you *don't* take even money. Let's assume a single deck, thus 49 cards remain of which 15 are 10s that will give the dealer blackjack:

$$E = \tfrac{15}{49} \times (0) + \tfrac{34}{49} \times (+1.5) = 1.04$$
$$\text{Player edge} = 104\%$$

Taking even money is a 100% return and that's nice. But a 104% return is even nicer. Why give up the 4% profit to the house?

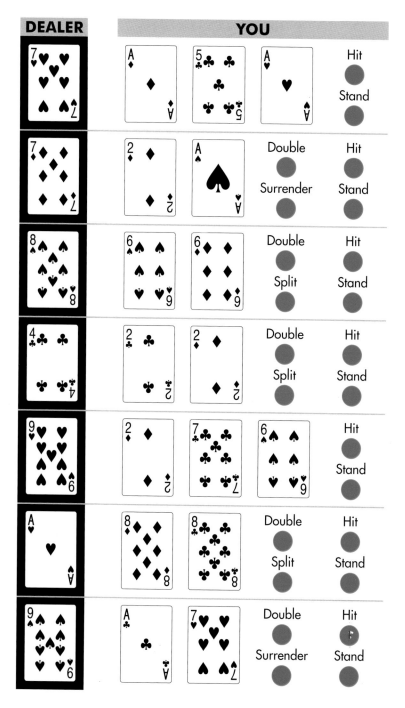

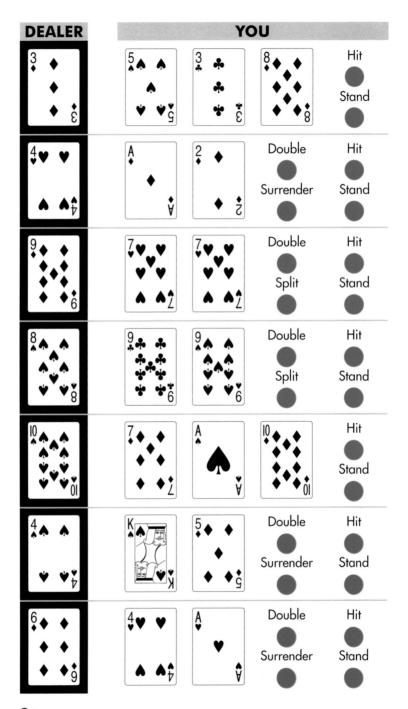

DEALER	YOU			
3♦	5♠	3♣	8♦	Hit / Stand
4♥	A♦	2♦		Double / Hit — Surrender / Stand
9♦	7♥	7♥		Double / Hit — Split / Stand
8♠	9♣	9♠		Double / Hit — Split / Stand
10♠	7♦	A♠	10♦	Hit / Stand
4♠	K♠	5♦		Double / Hit — Surrender / Stand
6♦	4♥	A♥		Double / Hit — Surrender / Stand

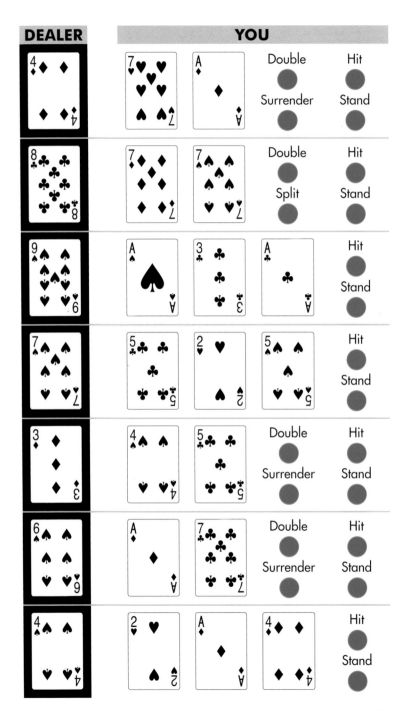

DEALER	YOU		
4♦	7♥	A♦	Double · Hit / Surrender · Stand
8♣	7♦	7♠	Double · Hit / Split · Stand
9♠	A♠	3♣ · A♣	Hit / Stand
7♠	5♣	2♥ · 5♠	Hit / Stand
3♦	4♠	5♣	Double · Hit / Surrender · Stand
6♠	A♦	7♣	Double · Hit / Surrender · Stand
4♠	2♥	A♦ · 4♦	Hit / Stand

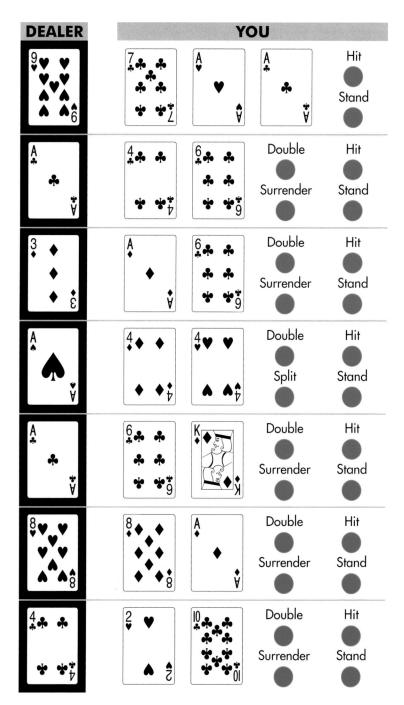

DEALER	YOU			
9♥ 6	7♣	A♥	A♣	Hit Stand
A♣	4♣	6♣	Double / Surrender	Hit / Stand
3♦	A♦	6♣	Double / Surrender	Hit / Stand
A♠	4♦	4♥	Double / Split	Hit / Stand
A♣	6♣	K♦	Double / Surrender	Hit / Stand
8♥	8♦	A♦	Double / Surrender	Hit / Stand
4♣	2♥	10♣	Double / Surrender	Hit / Stand

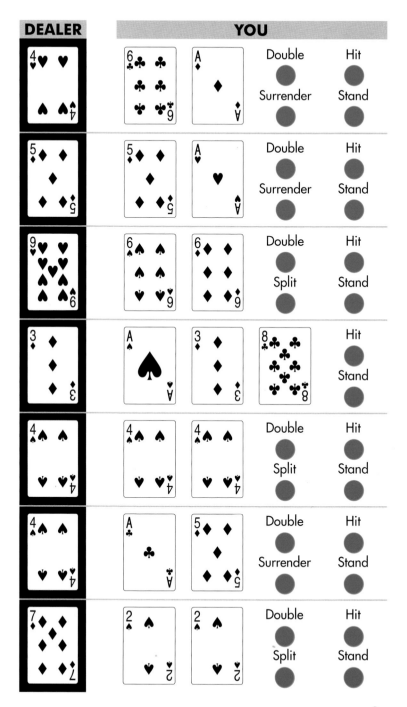

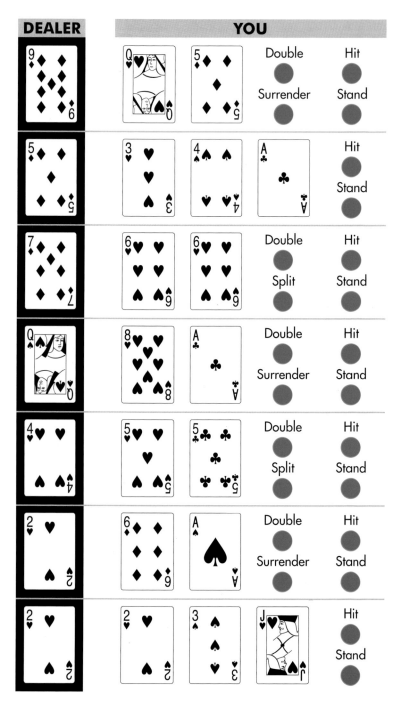

DEALER	YOU			
9♦	Q♥	5♦	Double / Surrender	Hit / Stand
5♦	3♥	4♠	A♣	Hit / Stand
7♦	6♥	6♥	Double / Split	Hit / Stand
Q♠	8♥	A♣	Double / Surrender	Hit / Stand
4♥	5♥	5♣	Double / Split	Hit / Stand
2♥	6♦	A♠	Double / Surrender	Hit / Stand
2♥	2♥	3♠	J♥	Hit / Stand

84

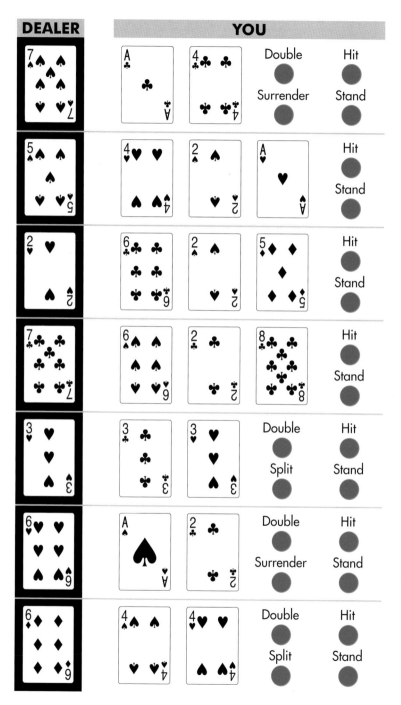

DEALER	YOU			
7♠	A♣	4♣	Double · Hit	
			Surrender · Stand	
5♠	4♥	2♠	A♥	Hit
				Stand
2♥	6♣	2♠	5♦	Hit
				Stand
7♣	6♠	2♣	8♣	Hit
				Stand
3♥	3♣	3♥	Double · Hit	
			Split · Stand	
6♥	A♠	2♣	Double · Hit	
			Surrender · Stand	
6♦	4♠	4♥	Double · Hit	
			Split · Stand	

85

DEALER	YOU			
A♥	A♣	5♣	A♠	Hit / Stand
9♥	A♦	4♣		Double / Surrender / Hit / Stand
K♦	6♥	A♣	A♠	Hit / Stand
6♥	2♥	3♣	A♥	Hit / Stand
A♦	5♠	5♦		Double / Split / Hit / Stand
7♦	7♥	7♦		Double / Split / Hit / Stand
6♣	5♥	3♥		Double / Surrender / Hit / Stand

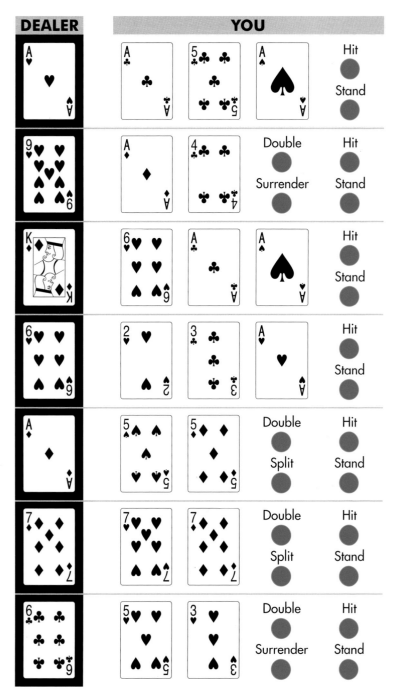

86

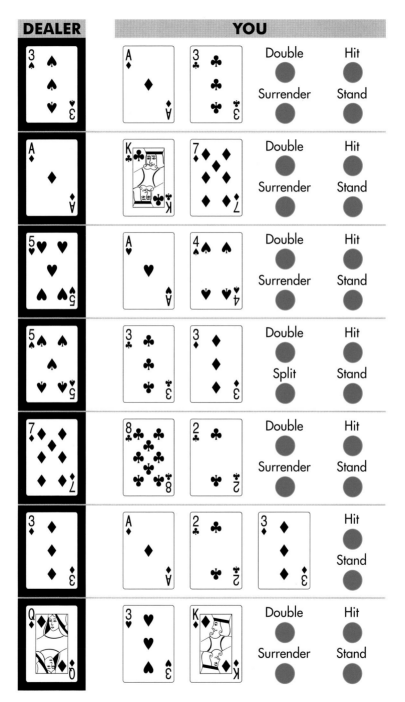

DEALER	YOU			
3 ♠	A ♦	3 ♣	Double · Hit ·	Surrender · Stand ·
A ♦	K ♣	7 ♦	Double · Hit ·	Surrender · Stand ·
5 ♥	A ♥	4 ♠	Double · Hit ·	Surrender · Stand ·
5 ♠	3 ♣	3 ♦	Double · Hit ·	Split · Stand ·
7 ♦	8 ♣	2 ♣	Double · Hit ·	Surrender · Stand ·
3 ♦	A ♦	2 ♣	3 ♦ Hit ·	Stand ·
Q ♦	3 ♥	K ♦	Double · Hit ·	Surrender · Stand ·

BETTING CHARTS

	2	3	4	5	6	7	8	9	10	Ace
8 or less	H	H	H	H	H	H	H	H	H	H
9	H	D	D	D	D	H	H	H	H	H
10	D	D	D	D	D	D	D	D	H	H
11	D	D	D	D	D	D	D	D	D	H
12	H	H	S	S	S	H	H	H	H	H
13	S	S	S	S	S	H	H	H	H	H
14	S	S	S	S	S	H	H	H	H	H
15	S	S	S	S	S	H	H	H	Rh	H
16	S	S	S	S	S	H	H	Rh	Rh	Rh
17–21	S	S	S	S	S	S	S	S	S	S

	2	3	4	5	6	7	8	9	10	Ace
Soft 13	H	H	H	D	D	H	H	H	H	H
Soft 14	H	H	H	D	D	H	H	H	H	H
Soft 15	H	H	D	D	D	H	H	H	H	H
Soft 16	H	H	D	D	D	H	H	H	H	H
Soft 17	H	D	D	D	D	H	H	H	H	H
Soft 18	S	Ds	Ds	Ds	Ds	S	S	H	H	H
Soft 19/20	S	S	S	S	S	S	S	S	S	S

	2	3	4	5	6	7	8	9	10	Ace
2,2	P	P	P	P	P	P	H	H	H	H
3,3	P	P	P	P	P	P	H	H	H	H
4,4	H	H	H	P	P	H	H	H	H	H
6,6	P	P	P	P	P	H	H	H	H	H
7,7	P	P	P	P	P	P	H	H	H	H
8,8	P	P	P	P	P	P	P	P	P	P
9,9	P	P	P	P	P	S	P	P	S	S
Ace,Ace	P	P	P	P	P	P	P	P	P	P

H	= Hit
S	= Stand
D	= Double if allowed, otherwise hit
Ds	= Double if allowed, otherwise stand
P	= Split
Rh	= Surrender if allowed, otherwise hit

- Always play 5,5 as 10.
- Always play 10,10 as 20.
- If you can't split because of a limit on resplitting, look up your hand as a hard total.
- Never take insurance or "even money."

4–8 DECKS, DEALER STANDS ON SOFT 17, NO DOUBLE AFTER SPLIT

	2	3	4	5	6	7	8	9	10	Ace
8 or less	H	H	H	H	H	H	H	H	H	H
9	H	D	D	D	D	H	H	H	H	H
10	D	D	D	D	D	D	D	D	H	H
11	D	D	D	D	D	D	D	D	D	H
12	H	H	S	S	S	H	H	H	H	H
13	S	S	S	S	S	H	H	H	H	H
14	S	S	S	S	S	H	H	H	H	H
15	S	S	S	S	S	H	H	H	Rh	H
16	S	S	S	S	S	H	H	Rh	Rh	Rh
17–21	S	S	S	S	S	S	S	S	S	S
	2	3	4	5	6	7	8	9	10	Ace
Soft 13	H	H	H	D	D	H	H	H	H	H
Soft 14	H	H	H	D	D	H	H	H	H	H
Soft 15	H	H	D	D	D	H	H	H	H	H
Soft 16	H	H	D	D	D	H	H	H	H	H
Soft 17	H	D	D	D	D	H	H	H	H	H
Soft 18	S	Ds	Ds	Ds	Ds	S	S	H	H	H
Soft 19/20	S	S	S	S	S	S	S	S	S	S
	2	3	4	5	6	7	8	9	10	Ace
2, 2	H	H	P	P	P	P	H	H	H	H
3, 3	H	H	P	P	P	P	H	H	H	H
4, 4	H	H	H	H	H	H	H	H	H	H
6, 6	H	P	P	P	P	H	H	H	H	H
7, 7	P	P	P	P	P	P	H	H	H	H
8, 8	P	P	P	P	P	P	P	P	P	P
9, 9	P	P	P	P	P	S	P	P	S	S
Ace, Ace	P	P	P	P	P	P	P	P	P	P

H = Hit
S = Stand
D = Double if allowed, otherwise hit
Ds = Double if allowed, otherwise stand
P = Split
Rh = Surrender if allowed, otherwise hit

- Always play 5, 5 as 10.
- Always play 10, 10 as 20.
- If you can't split because of a limit on resplitting, look up your hand as a hard total.
- Never take insurance or "even money."

4–8 DECKS, DEALER HITS SOFT 17, DOUBLE AFTER SPLIT

	2	3	4	5	6	7	8	9	10	Ace
8 or less	H	H	H	H	H	H	H	H	H	H
9	H	D	D	D	D	H	H	H	H	H
10	D	D	D	D	D	D	D	D	H	H
11	D	D	D	D	D	D	D	D	D	D
12	H	H	S	S	S	H	H	H	H	H
13	S	S	S	S	S	H	H	H	H	H
14	S	S	S	S	S	H	H	H	H	H
15	S	S	S	S	S	H	H	H	Rh	Rh
16	S	S	S	S	S	H	H	Rh	Rh	Rh
17	S	S	S	S	S	S	S	S	S	Rs
18–21	S	S	S	S	S	S	S	S	S	S

	2	3	4	5	6	7	8	9	10	Ace
Soft 13	H	H	H	D	D	H	H	H	H	H
Soft 14	H	H	H	D	D	H	H	H	H	H
Soft 15	H	H	D	D	D	H	H	H	H	H
Soft 16	H	H	D	D	D	H	H	H	H	H
Soft 17	H	D	D	D	D	H	H	H	H	H
Soft 18	Ds	Ds	Ds	Ds	Ds	S	S	H	H	H
Soft 19	S	S	S	S	Ds	S	S	S	S	S
Soft 20	S	S	S	S	S	S	S	S	S	S

	2	3	4	5	6	7	8	9	10	Ace
2, 2	P	P	P	P	P	P	H	H	H	H
3, 3	P	P	P	P	P	P	H	H	H	H
4, 4	H	H	H	P	P	H	H	H	H	H
6, 6	P	P	P	P	P	H	H	H	H	H
7, 7	P	P	P	P	P	P	H	H	H	H
8, 8	P	P	P	P	P	P	P	P	P	Rp
9, 9	P	P	P	P	P	S	P	P	S	S
Ace, Ace	P	P	P	P	P	P	P	P	P	P

H	= Hit
S	= Stand
D	= Double if allowed, otherwise hit
Ds	= Double if allowed, otherwise stand
P	= Split
Rh	= Surrender if allowed, otherwise hit
Rs	= Surrender if allowed, otherwise stand
Rp	= Surrender if allowed, otherwise split

- Always play 5, 5 as 10.
- Always play 10, 10 as 20.
- If you can't split because of a limit on resplitting, look up your hand as a hard total.
- Never take insurance or "even money."

4–8 DECKS, DEALER HITS SOFT 17, NO DOUBLE AFTER SPLIT

	2	3	4	5	6	7	8	9	10	Ace
8 or less	H	H	H	H	H	H	H	H	H	H
9	H	D	D	D	D	H	H	H	H	H
10	D	D	D	D	D	D	D	D	H	H
11	D	D	D	D	D	D	D	D	D	D
12	H	H	S	S	S	H	H	H	H	H
13	S	S	S	S	S	H	H	H	H	H
14	S	S	S	S	S	H	H	H	H	H
15	S	S	S	S	S	H	H	H	Rh	Rh
16	S	S	S	S	S	H	H	Rh	Rh	Rh
17	S	S	S	S	S	S	S	S	S	Rs
18–21	S	S	S	S	S	S	S	S	S	S

	2	3	4	5	6	7	8	9	10	Ace
Soft 13	H	H	H	D	D	H	H	H	H	H
Soft 14	H	H	H	D	D	H	H	H	H	H
Soft 15	H	H	D	D	D	H	H	H	H	H
Soft 16	H	H	D	D	D	H	H	H	H	H
Soft 17	H	D	D	D	D	H	H	H	H	H
Soft 18	Ds	Ds	Ds	Ds	Ds	S	S	H	H	H
Soft 19	S	S	S	S	Ds	S	S	S	S	S
Soft 20	S	S	S	S	S	S	S	S	S	S

	2	3	4	5	6	7	8	9	10	Ace
2, 2	H	H	P	P	P	P	H	H	H	H
3, 3	H	H	P	P	P	P	H	H	H	H
4, 4	H	H	H	H	H	H	H	H	H	H
6, 6	H	P	P	P	P	H	H	H	H	H
7, 7	P	P	P	P	P	P	H	H	H	H
8, 8	P	P	P	P	P	P	P	P	P	Rp
9, 9	P	P	P	P	P	S	P	P	S	S
Ace, Ace	P	P	P	P	P	P	P	P	P	P

H = Hit
S = Stand
D = Double if allowed, otherwise hit
Ds = Double if allowed, otherwise stand
P = Split
Rh = Surrender if allowed, otherwise hit
Rs = Surrender if allowed, otherwise stand
Rp = Surrender if allowed, otherwise split

- Always play 5, 5 as 10.
- Always play 10, 10 as 20.
- If you can't split because of a limit on resplitting, look up your hand as a hard total.
- Never take insurance or "even money."

SINGLE DECK, DEALER STANDS ON SOFT 17, DOUBLE AFTER SPLIT

	2	3	4	5	6	7	8	9	10	Ace
7 or less	H	H	H	H	H	H	H	H	H	H
8	H	H	H	D	D	H	H	H	H	H
9	D	D	D	D	D	H	H	H	H	H
10	D	D	D	D	D	D	D	D	H	H
11	D	D	D	D	D	D	D	D	D	D
12	H	H	S	S	S	H	H	H	H	H
13	S	S	S	S	S	H	H	H	H	H
14	S	S	S	S	S	H	H	H	H	H
15	S	S	S	S	S	H	H	H	H	H
16	S	S	S	S	S	H	H	H	Rh	Rh
17–21	S	S	S	S	S	S	S	S	S	S
	2	3	4	5	6	7	8	9	10	Ace
Soft 13	H	H	D	D	D	H	H	H	H	H
Soft 14	H	H	D	D	D	H	H	H	H	H
Soft 15	H	H	D	D	D	H	H	H	H	H
Soft 16	H	H	D	D	D	H	H	H	H	H
Soft 17	D	D	D	D	D	H	H	H	H	H
Soft 18	S	Ds	Ds	Ds	Ds	S	S	H	H	S
Soft 19	S	S	S	S	Ds	S	S	S	S	S
Soft 20	S	S	S	S	S	S	S	S	S	S
	2	3	4	5	6	7	8	9	10	Ace
2,2	P	P	P	P	P	P	H	H	H	H
3,3	P	P	P	P	P	P	P	H	H	H
4,4	H	H	P	P	P	H	H	H	H	H
6,6	P	P	P	P	P	P	H	H	H	H
7,7	P	P	P	P	P	P	P	H	Rs	H
8,8	P	P	P	P	P	P	P	P	P	P
9,9	P	P	P	P	P	S	P	P	S	S
Ace,Ace	P	P	P	P	P	P	P	P	P	P

H = Hit
S = Stand
D = Double if allowed, otherwise hit
Ds = Double if allowed, otherwise stand
P = Split
Rh = Surrender if allowed, otherwise hit
Rs = Surrender if allowed, otherwise stand

- Always play 5,5 as 10.
- Always play 10,10 as 20.
- If you can't split because of a limit on resplitting, look up your hand as a hard total.
- Never take insurance or "even money."

SINGLE DECK, DEALER STANDS ON SOFT 17, NO DOUBLE AFTER SPLIT

	2	3	4	5	6	7	8	9	10	Ace
7 or less	H	H	H	H	H	H	H	H	H	H
8	H	H	H	D	D	H	H	H	H	H
9	D	D	D	D	D	H	H	H	H	H
10	D	D	D	D	D	D	D	D	H	H
11	D	D	D	D	D	D	D	D	D	D
12	H	H	S	S	S	H	H	H	H	H
13	S	S	S	S	S	H	H	H	H	H
14	S	S	S	S	S	H	H	H	H	H
15	S	S	S	S	S	H	H	H	H	H
16	S	S	S	S	S	H	H	H	Rh	Rh
17–21	S	S	S	S	S	S	S	S	S	S
	2	3	4	5	6	7	8	9	10	Ace
Soft 13	H	H	D	D	D	H	H	H	H	H
Soft 14	H	H	D	D	D	H	H	H	H	H
Soft 15	H	H	D	D	D	H	H	H	H	H
Soft 16	H	H	D	D	D	H	H	H	H	H
Soft 17	D	D	D	D	D	H	H	H	H	H
Soft 18	S	Ds	Ds	Ds	Ds	S	S	H	H	S
Soft 19	S	S	S	S	Ds	S	S	S	S	S
Soft 20	S	S	S	S	S	S	S	S	S	S
	2	3	4	5	6	7	8	9	10	Ace
2,2	H	P	P	P	P	P	H	H	H	H
3,3	H	H	P	P	P	P	H	H	H	H
4,4	H	H	H	D	D	H	H	H	H	H
6,6	P	P	P	P	P	H	H	H	H	H
7,7	P	P	P	P	P	P	H	H	Rs	H
8,8	P	P	P	P	P	P	P	P	P	P
9,9	P	P	P	P	P	S	P	P	S	S
Ace, Ace	P	P	P	P	P	P	P	P	P	P

H = Hit
S = Stand
D = Double if allowed, otherwise hit
Ds = Double if allowed, otherwise stand
P = Split
Rh = Surrender if allowed, otherwise hit
Rs = Surrender if allowed, otherwise stand

- Always play 5, 5 as 10.
- Always play 10, 10 as 20.
- If you can't split because of a limit on resplitting, look up your hand as a hard total.
- Never take insurance or "even money."

SINGLE DECK, DEALER HITS ON SOFT 17, DOUBLE AFTER SPLIT

	2	3	4	5	6	7	8	9	10	Ace
7 or less	H	H	H	H	H	H	H	H	H	H
8	H	H	H	D	D	H	H	H	H	H
9	D	D	D	D	D	H	H	H	H	H
10	D	D	D	D	D	D	D	D	H	H
11	D	D	D	D	D	D	D	D	D	D
12	H	H	S	S	S	H	H	H	H	H
13	S	S	S	S	S	H	H	H	H	H
14	S	S	S	S	S	H	H	H	H	H
15	S	S	S	S	S	H	H	H	H	Rh
16	S	S	S	S	S	H	H	H	Rh	Rh
17	S	S	S	S	S	S	S	S	S	Rs
18–21	S	S	S	S	S	S	S	S	S	S

	2	3	4	5	6	7	8	9	10	Ace
Soft 13	H	H	D	D	D	H	H	H	H	H
Soft 14	H	H	D	D	D	H	H	H	H	H
Soft 15	H	H	D	D	D	H	H	H	H	H
Soft 16	H	H	D	D	D	H	H	H	H	H
Soft 17	D	D	D	D	D	H	H	H	H	H
Soft 18	S	Ds	Ds	Ds	Ds	S	S	H	H	H
Soft 19	S	S	S	S	Ds	S	S	S	S	S
Soft 20	S	S	S	S	S	S	S	S	S	S

	2	3	4	5	6	7	8	9	10	Ace
2,2	P	P	P	P	P	P	H	H	H	H
3,3	P	P	P	P	P	P	P	H	H	H
4,4	H	H	P	P	P	H	H	H	H	H
6,6	P	P	P	P	P	P	H	H	H	H
7,7	P	P	P	P	P	P	P	H	Rs	Rh
8,8	P	P	P	P	P	P	P	P	P	P
9,9	P	P	P	P	P	S	P	P	S	P
Ace, Ace	P	P	P	P	P	P	P	P	P	P

H = Hit
S = Stand
D = Double if allowed, otherwise hit
Ds = Double if allowed, otherwise stand
P = Split
Rh = Surrender if allowed, otherwise hit
Rs = Surrender if allowed, otherwise stand

- Always play 5, 5 as 10.
- Always play 10, 10 as 20.
- If you can't split because of a limit on resplitting, look up your hand as a hard total.
- Never take insurance or "even money."

SINGLE DECK, DEALER HITS ON SOFT 17, NO DOUBLE AFTER SPLIT

	2	3	4	5	6	7	8	9	10	Ace
7 or less	H	H	H	H	H	H	H	H	H	H
8	H	H	H	D	D	H	H	H	H	H
9	D	D	D	D	D	H	H	H	H	H
10	D	D	D	D	D	D	D	D	H	H
11	D	D	D	D	D	D	D	D	D	D
12	H	H	S	S	S	H	H	H	H	H
13	S	S	S	S	S	H	H	H	H	H
14	S	S	S	S	S	H	H	H	H	H
15	S	S	S	S	S	H	H	H	H	Rh
16	S	S	S	S	S	H	H	H	Rh	Rh
17	S	S	S	S	S	S	S	S	S	Rs
18–21	S	S	S	S	S	S	S	S	S	S

	2	3	4	5	6	7	8	9	10	Ace
Soft 13	H	H	D	D	D	H	H	H	H	H
Soft 14	H	H	D	D	D	H	H	H	H	H
Soft 15	H	H	D	D	D	H	H	H	H	H
Soft 16	H	H	D	D	D	H	H	H	H	H
Soft 17	D	D	D	D	D	H	H	H	H	H
Soft 18	S	Ds	Ds	Ds	Ds	S	S	H	H	H
Soft 19	S	S	S	S	Ds	S	S	S	S	S
Soft 20	S	S	S	S	S	S	S	S	S	S

	2	3	4	5	6	7	8	9	10	Ace
2,2	H	P	P	P	P	P	H	H	H	H
3,3	H	H	P	P	P	P	H	H	H	H
4,4	H	H	H	D	D	H	H	H	H	H
6,6	P	P	P	P	P	H	H	H	H	H
7,7	P	P	P	P	P	P	H	H	Rs	Rh
8,8	P	P	P	P	P	P	P	P	P	P
9,9	P	P	P	P	P	S	P	P	S	S
Ace,Ace	P	P	P	P	P	P	P	P	P	P

H = Hit
S = Stand
D = Double if allowed, otherwise hit
Ds = Double if allowed, otherwise stand
P = Split
Rh = Surrender if allowed, otherwise hit
Rs = Surrender if allowed, otherwise stand

- Always play 5, 5 as 10.
- Always play 10, 10 as 20.
- If you can't split because of a limit on resplitting, look up your hand as a hard total.
- Never take insurance or "even money."

ABOUT THE AUTHOR

ANDREW BRISMAN is the author of the *Mensa Guide to Casino Gambling* which the *Detroit Free Press* declared "the runaway winner as the best overall gambling encyclopedia written in the past 20 years." The *Mensa Guide* is consistently mentioned as one of the top gambling guides and has been used as a textbook at several colleges.

A former editor at *Games* magazine and *Nickelodeon Magazine*, Brisman has produced hundreds of games and puzzles for adults and children. He started playing at the casino blackjack tables before he had a legal right to do so. Aside from a brief period as a mediocre card counter, he has never taken insurance and has always hit 16 against dealer's 7.

Brisman and his wife live in New York City with their two young sons, both of whom employ the basic strategy of throwing their cards in the air when they're done playing.